THE MAGIC OF IMPERFECTION

THE MAGIC OF IMPERFECTION

The ¾ Baked Secret to Unlocking Innovation
and Getting More Done

JASON F. MCLENNAN

Berrett–Koehler Publishers, Inc.

Berrett-Koehler Publishers, Inc.
1333 Broadway, Suite P100
Oakland, CA 94612-1921
Tel: (510) 817-2277
Fax: (510) 817-2278
bkconnection.com

ORDERING INFORMATION

Quantity sales. Special discounts are available on quantity purchases by corporations, associations, and others. For details, please go to bkconnection.com to see our bulk discounts or contact bookorders@bkpub.com for more information.

Individual sales. Berrett-Koehler publications are available through most bookstores. They can also be ordered directly from Berrett-Koehler: Tel: (800) 929-2929; Fax: (802) 864-7626; bkconnection.com.

Orders for college textbook / course adoption use. Please contact Berrett-Koehler:
Tel: (800) 929-2929; Fax: (802) 864-7626.

Distributed to the US trade and internationally by Penguin Random House Publisher Services.

The authorized representative in the EU for product safety and compliance is
EU Compliance Partner, Pärnu mnt. 139b-14, 11317 Tallinn, Estonia,
www.eucompliancepartner.com, +372 5368 65 02.

Berrett-Koehler and the BK logo are registered trademarks of Berrett-Koehler Publishers, Inc.

Printed in Canada

Berrett-Koehler books are printed on long-lasting acid-free paper. When it is available, we choose paper that has been manufactured by environmentally responsible processes. These may include using trees grown in sustainable forests, incorporating recycled paper, minimizing chlorine in bleaching, or recycling the energy produced at the paper mill.

Library of Congress Control Number: 2025007692
ISBN 9798890571014 (paperback) | ISBN 9798890571021 (pdf) |
ISBN 9798890571038 (epub)

First Edition
33 32 31 30 29 28 27 26 25   10 9 8 7 6 5 4 3 2 1

Book production: Happenstance Type-O-Rama
Cover design: Ashley Ingram

This book is dedicated to all the four-legged family that have played such an important part of my life and my family's life over the years: Melinka, Samantha, Athena, Papillon (Pappy), Luna, Sammie, Archibald (Archie), and North.

Our lives have been enriched by their love and devotion.

CONTENTS

ODE TO THE ¾ BAKED COOKIE

I LOOK IN THE OVEN at the cookies baking inside.

Mouth watering, I prepare to eat the perfect mix of cooked dough and chocolate chips . . . with a glass of cold milk, of course.

But why are the windows into ovens always so crappy? Peering through the dimly lit interior, I try to gauge color and firmness. . . .

Not wanting to open the oven too soon and upset the delicate thermal balance, I try to guess the right moment to take the cookies out.

Too soon, and they are gooey and undercooked. Too late, and the bottom burns and the cookies dry out; once cooled, they are inedible as far as I am concerned.

And they keep cooking! The pan remains hot after emerging and the cookies continue to firm—it is not so straightforward as the recipe suggests, if you believe that so much delight is at stake.

So I have learned from experience to take my cookies out when ¾ baked, and to let the universe finish what I have begun. I can watch them become perfect in the light of day and then enjoy how flour, sugar, salt, eggs, butter, and chocolate can come together . . . like a sacred thing.

PREFACE

AUTHORS SHOULD NEVER WRITE a book if they're not clear about who it's for.

I think this book is for you!

Why you?

Well, I can guess that this book was given to you by someone who knows you well or found its way to you because you have important work to do, important ideas to share, and important causes to support. You wish to do things that matter.

When you are mission driven, you always need to know how to be more effective and impactful.

That's easier said than done, it seems.

And even if you are not overly mission driven and you just want to know how to get more done without so much effort and stress—perhaps to have more time for family and recreation—well, that's okay too, as this book can help you radically, almost magically, increase your output over time as you apply its lessons.

Life has a habit of getting in the way. We never seem to have enough time to dedicate to the things we love, and we so often get bogged down with efforts that are not advancing our careers, our education, our mission, or things we care about. We all struggle with time management and not having enough time—period.

Why is it so hard to just get things done?

How would you like to radically accelerate your ability to get work done with significantly greater effectiveness—all while having more time left over for other things you care about?

If this sounds attractive—then, yes, this book is for you.

This book is intended to help you increase your "success rate" so that you can achieve the goals and aspirations you've set out for yourself.

It will show you how to more effectively make time both for work and for the things and people you love by changing your mindset and your process for getting things done.

My Mission of Change

When I started my career, I decided that I wanted to dedicate my life to creating positive change using architecture and design as my tools of trade. My love for the environment and its many glorious, rare, and beautiful creatures motivates me to look for solutions for how we live, work, and build that upend the trajectory of modern architecture and city-making, which often puts the built environment at odds with the natural environment. Each day, I work to create buildings and environments that can be "regenerative" and work as levers for healing the environment. I have designed many buildings, for example, that run only on solar power, operate nearly pollution free, and work solely with the water that falls on their rooftops, along the way creating exceptional habitats for both people and other living things—buildings I call *Living Buildings* because they prioritize life.

I have written several books about this topic and continue to practice with an incredible team of architects, engineers, scientists, and designers doing projects all over the world. But that is not what this book is about. In fact, this book isn't about architecture at all—it's a book for anyone who wants to become more effective and innovative in any work they do.

This book is about how, despite increasing headwinds, you can get massive quantities of things done efficiently in service to your personal mission every year using a very particular philosophy of change I have developed: the ¾ baked secret. Its core tenets are based on some of these things I've learned over time:

- It's not enough to simply work hard. Lots of people work hard. To be a changemaker, you must match your strategic efforts with *clarity*.

- It's not enough to be talented either. Lots of people are talented as well. You have to find ways to express and harness your talent through continuous feedback in order to hone and fine-tune it so that the talent becomes *effective*.

- Working effectively means working very differently than how most people tend to work, upending conventional approaches to productivity, collaboration, and risk-taking. Working effectively requires a *new mindset* and way of seeing the world.

- Getting things done is a *discipline*, and by focusing on what is essential and minimizing time spent on what is not (and knowing how to tell the difference), you can create dramatic shifts in productivity.

With the ¾ baked secret, you can become highly effective, prolific, and efficient in anything you do, whether it is architecture, business, music, writing, or some other creative or non-creative pursuit. This book will help leaders, managers, entrepreneurs, students, and doers of any kind be more productive and innovative.

Through a lot of practice and trial and error, I've also developed a whole theory of productivity. I call it ¾ *baked thinking*, and it's what this book is based on. When people use ¾ baked thinking effectively, they can get remarkable amounts of work done—at a high quality—in a short amount of time by harnessing a form of magical imperfection.

And you can do this too!

Your Turn!

Maybe you marvel at those who somehow manage to get a lot done. I bet they've learned the ¾ baked secret of the magic of imperfection.

I love when people ask me, "How do you get so much done?!" They're amazed at how I constantly and seemingly effortlessly generate ideas and results, without realizing that they, too, can become just as effective and efficient, if they only approach things a little differently.

This book tells you how.

You can't strike out if you don't get up to bat in life—or, as Babe Ruth once said, "Never let the fear of striking out keep you from playing the game."

INTRODUCTION

The ¾ Baked Recipe for Success

An army of sheep, led by a lion, is better
than an army of lions, led by a sheep.

—ALEXANDER THE GREAT

OVER THREE DECADES, I've had the great pleasure of working with and being an advisor to many of the world's top companies and institutions. I have worked with several dozen universities all over North America—from Canada to Mexico, including venerable institutions like Yale, Vanderbilt, and Georgia Tech. I have worked with companies that have more revenue than many small countries do and make many of the things we use in our daily lives, from computers and airplanes to the stone, tile, wood, and carpet that we use to build our homes. I have had clients who are billionaires, celebrities, and prospective US presidents. I have worked with governments at the national, state, and local levels across the United States and Canada. I have also worked with small non-profits, First Nation tribes, and business startups with only a handful of employees.

And from all this experience, I have learned that innovation and effectiveness do not always track in ways that people think.

I have been a careful observer of how entities of all types—from big to small, complex to simple—get things done or struggle to do so. In the end, regardless of the organization and its voracity to change the world, **people** and **how they think** are the most important or most harmful attribute. People and process are both the numerator and denominator in the equation of success and failure.

For example, one massive company that I consulted to had shockingly outdated ways of thinking and working, as well as a culture of "paralysis by analysis" with high-paid, talented staff who were afraid to stick their necks out on anything. Therefore, very little, aside from incremental improvements, ever got done. This is a company that was once one of the world's most innovative and influential businesses and that still supplies hugely important products for societies all over the world—but does so now with shockingly outdated and rundown facilities, a culture of inefficiency, and risk aversion. Many people assume that the biggest and most important organizations are also the best at what they do, and yet this is often not the case.

On an individual level, it's also easy to assume that it is always the smartest and most talented individuals who are the most effective. Remember the straight-A students from your high school who seemed destined for greatness? A large number of them end up with only modest or average societal and economic contributions. Great talent and intelligence are obviously advantages, but by themselves they're easily undermined by critical flaws in approach, attitude, and personal philosophy. We've all been around smart people who can't seem to get out of their own way or are so self-critical that they can't get anything done.

Perhaps you wonder why *you* can't get more done or have a bigger impact in your work and life. If so, you're in the right place. This book contains an entirely new philosophy on life and business that has the capacity to unlock your potential and significantly improve your capabilities to innovate and, even more exciting, how quickly you innovate. It involves an almost magical concept of avoiding perfection and perfectionist thinking (the opposite of what most people try to do) and seeking to release things at a certain point in their imperfect quest for rapid feedback and then iteration. The "magic" to achieving perfection, in other words, is to *avoid* seeking it and learn to embrace imperfections in a way that ironically actually gets you closer to it, and faster.

I call this magic approach ¾ *baked thinking*, and, if properly applied and practiced, it will improve your projects' success rate, your workflow, and even aspects of your personal life, saving you time and perhaps even making you a lot happier and less stressed.

But as with anything else in life, new challenges and expectations typically require new ways of doing things. Success requires letting go of old habits, recognizing and shifting established patterns, and embracing a few simple yet fundamental ideas. It also requires a willingness to fail fast and learn from that experience in order to apply that new knowledge appropriately to your situation and context.

Mise en Place

Let me share a metaphor.

Good chefs take the time to prepare their ingredients so that when heat is applied, everything is ready, and there's less risk of overcooking or undercooking the food. This process, known as *mise en place* (French for "putting in place" or "gathering ingredients"), is not only about preparation, but also about *enjoying the act of* preparation.

Mise en place is a useful metaphor for this book. You can think of each chapter as a different ingredient that is required to make the overall recipe—the ¾ baked philosophy—successful.

Let's go a bit deeper with this metaphor.

Imagine an unpracticed home chef who cooks spaghetti by dumping it into a big pot and letting it boil away until the pasta seems ready to eat. After all, it even says on the box how long to cook it! They foolishly try to get it perfectly cooked while it still boils, when, in reality, it is now on its way to becoming overcooked. The home cook takes their "ready to eat" pasta out, strains it through a colander, and then lets it sit while they finish the sauce, which they've removed from the jar and let simmer. To plate the food, the home cook simply pours the sauce on top of a pile of spaghetti. Voilà!

The result is typically far from satisfactory: the hot pasta continues to cook in the colander and becomes sticky and mushy, and the sauce simply sits on top of it, ensuring bites with too little or too much sauce.

How uncivilized.

Consider a more sophisticated approach by a seasoned chef. Ahead of cooking the pasta, the chef prepares their mise en place. Then, only when the ingredients are ready, the chef makes a simple homemade sauce with olive oil, garlic, fresh tomatoes, Parmesan, and seasonings. Despite its simplicity, it's a more thoughtful preparation than that of the home cook.

The chef then places the pasta in boiling water, cooking it only until it is ¾ finished—slightly firmer than al dente. This is essential. The chef is not trying to cook the pasta fully in the water but instead looking for the "sweet spot" where the pasta has absorbed enough heat to be mostly cooked. At that point, they remove the pasta and finish cooking it directly in the sauce.

Thanks to this key step—at a ¾ point—a couple of things happen:

- Since it's not fully done, the pasta can rehydrate and absorb the sauce as it finishes cooking, ensuring even flavor distribution and infusion into the noodles. This is akin to sharing your ideas with the world early and letting other people's ideas and market feedback infuse and perfect it—a core part of my philosophy.

- Because the pasta can no longer stick to itself, each strand is separated and bound by sauce, not gluten—a good metaphor for not getting stuck in one place and rigid in our ways (another key tenet).

Same ingredients, but different process—the result of which is most assuredly a vastly superior meal.

- - -

In this book, you'll learn about several important principles and skills:

- The world is full of half-baked ideas that are no good to anyone. Properly preparing, testing, and refining ideas and work product through rapid feedback ensures that they can be as successful as possible and never half-baked.

- The world is full of overcooked and burnt ideas past their prime that never get out of the kitchen or out of your inbox. It's important to recognize when you are holding onto ideas too long, being too much of a perfectionist, insisting on controlling every detail, or undermining your own or others' success by not observing timely, well-planned deadlines.

- The act of sharing at the magical ¾ baked moment tends to create a culture of innovation and collaboration where the skills of the many enhance those of the few.

- Harnessing feedback and failure encourages a process of constant improvement for yourself and your team. The ¾ baked way can be perfected like an art form!

- You can effectively apportion your efforts so that there's always time for the important things in your life and you become known as someone who can be counted on to consistently deliver.

- Aligning your passion with what you do at work will yield greater satisfaction, personal benefit, and ultimately happiness.

These lessons and key takeaways from each chapter are summarized in features labeled "¾ Baked Secret," which appear throughout the book.

We all have dreams and aspirations to accomplish in our lives, but so often our work and life "stuff" just gets in the way. Our life energy is precious, and we should spend it where it matters, not waste it where it doesn't. So let's get cooking to find out how!

CHAPTER 1

Avoiding the Chase for Perfection

The artist who aims at perfection in everything achieves it in nothing.

— EUGÈNE DELACROIX

AS ODD AS IT MAY SOUND, I've always tried *not* to seek perfection — at least most of the time. Don't get me wrong: I always give my best effort and work hard at whatever I do. I believe wholeheartedly in committing myself to each task I face and devoting all my knowledge and energy to the job at hand if that's what's required. But . . . I've also learned when to stop. I've trained myself to recognize the point at which my continued efforts might hinder a project's progress, the point when it is time to release my work into the world to allow other individuals or forces to complete it or, at a minimum, to provide critical feedback.

This is the stage I refer to as ¾ baked.

When we refer to something as "half-baked," we often mean that it's inadequate or incomplete. The phrase has a negative implication. To extend the culinary metaphor, a half-baked item is undercooked; it is certainly unappetizing, and possibly hazardous. Half-baked chicken is not a thing in restaurants for good reason. And we also tend to know when something is overbaked — the idea or project is "cooked" well past its time, leading to blown deadlines and missed opportunities. This is akin to food that is burnt and inedible. Lazy people consistently put out half-baked ideas because they can't be bothered to care enough to put in more effort. Perfectionists care too much in unhealthy ways, and therefore often overcook their ideas and hesitate to share them out into the world.

When I talk about an idea or task being ¾ baked, I mean that it has reached a moment in time or point in development where it has significant shape, clarity, and elegance to be understood as a product or deliverable, but it's still imperfect. It can stand on its own, perfectly workable, yet it still has room for improvement—some rough edges to hone and questions to resolve. When a concept is ¾ baked, its original author or "architect" has taken it to a stage of near completion and then, resisting the urge to keep refining, has offered it up to the outside world for feedback, criticism, and testing.

Oddly enough, aiming for this stage of development, rather than striving for perfection, is likely to bring about a more perfect result. This is the core message of this book. Cultivating a sense of where this sweet spot resides is the magic key to get radically more work done at a higher level of quality. Aiming to share not at the point of perfection but at the ¾ baked moment is a powerful and critical distinction.

Consider the Goal: Be Wary of Perfectionists!

In my opinion, when people strive to work on things to the point of perfection, they are usually fooling themselves and getting caught up either in their ego or in a self-doubt/self-critical feedback loop. Perfectionists spend so much time and energy making miniscule improvements and redoing perfectly fine work that they often end up losing sight of the ultimate goals of the projects they tackle. We've all heard the statistic that 90 percent of our efforts are expended on 10 percent of the result. It's usually the last 10 percent or the last 25 percent that does us in and keeps good ideas from going somewhere. The 80/20 rule is another way of saying something similar. So do not fall into that trap! Deliberately work to a point where you can share what you've done even when you know it needs work—that's the key.

When I studied in Glasgow, Scotland, I had a classmate who was an incredibly talented architectural designer. The only problem was that he always aimed for perfection in everything he did. He would work endlessly on something and never knew how to let go; he could not move on until it was perfect, which meant that he rarely moved on at all. He consistently produced beautiful artifacts, but he never completed them. Regardless of the assignment and its importance, he put in the same amount of effort and placed the same amount of pressure on himself. As a result, he suffered greatly from stress, even over assignments that were inconsequential. This is a lesson we will come back to: not everything is a big deal. He had been taught by his parents, I can only assume, to pursue perfection at all costs; indeed, to equate his own value as a person with how close to perfect his accomplishments were.

Because he did not know how to stop and be satisfied, each assignment was a huge challenge for him. Being human, he repeatedly produced things that were less than perfect. Not surprisingly, his self-esteem suffered greatly. He had never learned the valuable lesson of scaling effort to the importance of the task at hand. Nobody had taught him that chasing perfection was a fool's errand. Nobody had taught him that his value as a person wasn't tied directly to everything he worked on. By the end of the year, my friend was close to failing due to the number of assignments he simply could not complete, even though he had more talent than just about anyone else in our class. He refused to move on with one element of an assignment until he deemed it perfect, at which point he simply ran out of time to finish the rest or became immobilized by the self-generated pressure. The sad thing was that the quality of his work was higher than just about anyone's in our year—but he was his own worst enemy. In trying to go for a home run each time, he never scored a single hit.

I'm sure you know people like this, or perhaps you recognize this tendency in yourself.

Later in life, I became friends with a man who was an amazing trumpet player. From a young age, he showed talent that his father (as well as his teachers) spotted as real potential. In his efforts to encourage his son, the father ended up instilling an unhealthy set of expectations focused on being "perfect." As my friend got older, he stopped playing music altogether. I assumed that he quit because he no longer enjoyed the trumpet, but he told me that he loved the instrument and missed it terribly. However, he gave it up when family and work obligations limited his practice time to what he perceived as an unacceptable level, and he began to hear nothing but his mistakes. For him, this artistic pursuit was all or nothing; he felt he needed to be perfect or not play at all. In his case, a quest for perfection killed the music in this man, and I believe that his life was less rich as a result.

One of the secrets to success is knowing when to stop—how hard to work and for how long. I have seen so many great talents waste their skills on the hubris of perfection.

In so many disciplines, the perfect is the enemy of the good. People obsess over details, worrying about acceptance, approval, and propriety. By the time they finish an endeavor, the reality has often changed, making their deliberations all for naught. I have watched as skilled professionals have blown projects not by underperforming but by overthinking to the point where they missed deadlines or exceeded budgets. Show me a perfectionist, and I will show you someone who does not get much done.

People throw away what they could have
by insisting on perfection, which they
cannot have, and looking for it where they
will never find it.

— EDITH SCHAEFFER

The greater the emphasis on perfection,
the further it recedes.

— HARIDAS CHAUDHURI

¾ BAKED SECRET

In any endeavor, scale the effort of your work to the effort required for success.

Accept that sometimes your "best" varies under different conditions.

Do not overthink or overdo.

Achieve success by practicing balance and restraint without harsh internal judgment.

The Sweet Spot

The thing that is really hard, and really amazing, is giving up on being perfect and beginning the work of becoming yourself.

—ANNA QUINDLEN

How do we seek and identify the ¾ baked sweet spot of our own undertakings? How do we give ourselves permission to be less than perfect, while demanding from ourselves more than mediocrity? How do we embrace the "magic of imperfection"?

Often, when I am seeking my own answers to life's dilemmas, I cook. I find that cooking provides many lessons applicable to our lives and the decisions we must make. Releasing a project when it is ¾ baked is a lot like preparing asparagus. If you steam fresh asparagus until it is "perfectly cooked," it will end up overdone and soggy by the time you eat it. Why? Because, just like pasta, it continues to cook as long as it is hot, and there's a very fine line between deliciously al dente and horribly mushy. An experienced chef knows to remove the asparagus from the hot water when it is about ¾ cooked. Some push a little past ¾ done but plunge it into cold water immediately after removing it from the heat. In either case, the universe (in the form of cold water or the absence of hot water) finishes the job to help accomplish crunchy but cooked excellence.

When we put something out in the world—an idea, a design, a project—we must be willing to accept that it likely isn't perfect. So why fight this reality? Why not embrace it and use it to get more done and to get more feedback? When we are open to possible changes and criticisms and invite others to expand upon our original vision, we give our work and ourselves a great gift. When we hold on to an idea too long as we pursue its perfect execution, we run the risk of squeezing the life right out of it. Overcooked ideas are ones that lose their freshness and no longer produce desirable outcomes.

So, an idea's sweet spot—the time and place at which it is ¾ baked—is the magical point between its conception and its death by strangulation. If you truly wish to be effective in business and life, you must learn how to recognize and cultivate this sweet spot (see Figure 1.1).

If You Love It, Set It Free

When we release our ideas into the ether, magical transformations can take place. It takes courage to let go of our biggest and boldest work, especially when doing so requires acknowledging imperfections and possibilities for error. But taking that chance often leads to great things—magical things, even—when the ideas are good enough to take on a life of their own.

The universe, it seems, will provide what is required when we allow it to, doing away with bad ideas (usually for everyone's benefit) and elevating good ones. The individual who conceives the idea, and is strong enough to release it fully when it is ¾ baked, enables the world to

- determine whether the idea is worthy,

- strengthen the idea and help it shine more brightly,

- focus on the idea rather than the author, and

- remember that letting go of ego can be the best idea of all.

STAGES OF DEVELOPMENT

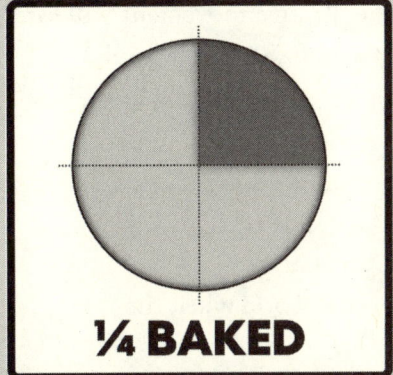

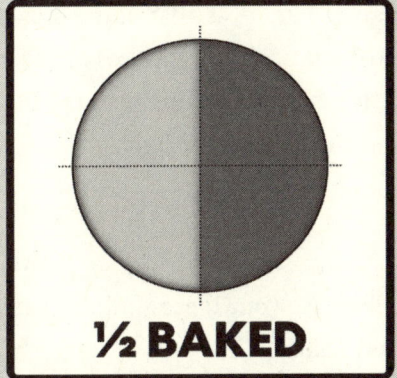

¼ baked is the beginning of any project or task, a magical moment of imperfection when you should be testing ideas and trying to understand the essence and endgame of any assignment.

½ baked is the messy middle of any project or task when the work should be tested and evaluated. Is it any good? Is it worth pursuing? Should the work stop or be reshaped, or can it be made excellent with more effort?

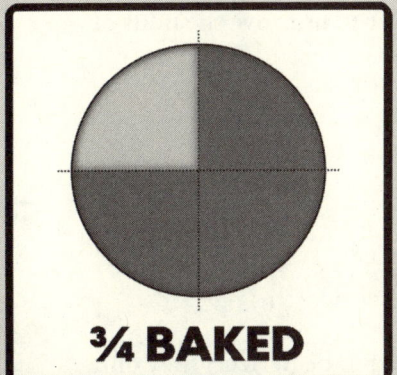

¾ baked is the "magic of imperfection" moment when an idea has clarity and coherence and can and should be shared out with the world for further refinement. Once it's ¾ baked, it is developed enough to be evaluated and refined by others on its own terms. It is not perfect, but it is perfectly imperfect.

Fully baked is an imaginary or elusive state when something is perfect— usually as a result of contributions by many and refinements over time. Can you really think of something that is perfect?

FIGURE 1.1: The four stages of development.

After all, if it is change we seek, we need not concern ourselves with glory. Work released in the right spirit tends to find ways to reward its creator. The ideas that come out of the collective movement will safeguard our future, regardless of how or by whom they are created. Releasing ideas into the universe in the spirit of selfless passion for change results in powerful magic.

¾ BAKED SECRET

Release your ideas and innovations to the world when they are ¾ baked.

Learn when to stop and invite others to contribute and collaborate.

Resist the urge to constantly refine and iterate until something is "perfect" before sharing.

Remember that chasing perfection is a fool's errand.

Let go instead of hanging on in order to improve the odds of achieving perfection.

¾ BAKED SECRET

Never equate your work with your self-worth.

Resist negative self-talk and the need to be perfect; they only take you further away from ever achieving perfection.

Avoid getting too emotionally attached to your work, which blinds you from how to actually improve it.

Cut yourself some slack and share early and often, in a spirit of generosity rather than ego.

The Living Building Challenge

Since the mid-1990s, I have been focused on a concept that I call *Living Buildings*. I coined the term while working on a project in Montana called the EpiCenter, as our team sought to describe building performance that was "truly sustainable." The idea is that nature, not machines, provides the ideal metaphor for the buildings of the future.

What is a Living Building? Imagine a building designed and constructed to function as elegantly and efficiently as a flower, one that is informed specifically by place, climate, topography, and microclimate. Imagine buildings that generate all their own energy with renewable resources; capture, treat, and reuse water in a closed-loop process; operate pollution-free with no toxic chemicals used in any material—all while being a beautiful inspiration to anyone who interacts with them. Even before LEED (Leadership in Energy and Environmental Design, the industry benchmark) came to fruition, my colleagues and I spent hours focusing on how to develop the Living Building idea, eventually publishing a series of articles on the subject. Back then, it was always only a fuzzy concept—a vague notion of the kind of impact we wanted buildings to have.

In 2005, I was encouraged by the strides that the green building industry was finally making. I had worked on two Platinum LEED projects and two Gold LEED projects, all of which were completed on budget and on time, and I was convinced that the industry was ready to go deeper. So, in my spare time in the evenings and on weekends, I began working on codifying what a Living Building needed to do to deserve the designation. I finished the first version of the Living Building Challenge (Figure 1.2) while moving out to Seattle to start as the new CEO of the Cascadia Region Green Building Council in the summer of 2006 (Cascadia eventually became the International Living Future Institute). I knew that what I had on my hands was a special document, but I also understood that it was far from perfect. As defined on the International

Living Future Institute's website (Living-Future.org), the Living Building Challenge is

> a philosophy, advocacy tool, and certification program defining today's most advanced measure of sustainability in the built environment. It addresses all buildings at all scales and is an inclusive tool for transformative design. Whether the project is a single building, a renovation, an infrastructure project, or a park, the Living Building Challenge provides a framework for designing, constructing, and improving the symbiotic relationships between people and all aspects of the built and natural environments.

It was a powerful idea—¾ baked—and ready to be shared with the industry. I decided to bring the intellectual property to Cascadia and to give it away without asking for any compensation. It had too much potential to be "owned" by a single individual, and the spirit of the tool demanded that personal profit could not be a motivator in releasing the work. But there was an important condition: when I offered the tool to the organization's board of directors, I told them that they could have it if we made it a centerpiece in the organization's future. They accepted, and that decision started a chain of powerful and positive outcomes.

Any good idea needs three things: the right timing, the right message, and the right platform. With Cascadia, all three began to align to make the Living Building Challenge a reality (see Figure 1.2). Pulling some strings with friends at the US Green Building Council, Bob Berkebile (my mentor that I'll introduce later) and I united to present the idea at the 2006 GreenBuild (the largest green building conference

FIGURE 1.2: The Living Building Challenge logo, which is based on the imperfect perfection of a flower. (Source: International Living Future Institute.)

in the world) in Denver to a crowd of several thousand leading practitioners. Opening right before my childhood hero, David Suzuki, we asked the assembled delegation to join us in "accepting the Challenge." In a moment that will always remain a powerful personal milestone for me, the whole assembly rose in a spontaneous standing ovation. Releasing a ¾ baked idea had started a paradigm shift in the building industry.

Since then, what has happened has been truly phenomenal: hundreds of projects have emerged all over North America and beyond, racing to be the first Living Buildings in their respective markets. Now, Living Buildings exist in many communities as living proof of what is possible.

These buildings will provide critical models for how people will live, work, and play in the coming decades, finally reconciling the balance between the natural and built environments. Thousands of people from many different disciplines—most of whom I have never even met—are now working to advance the ideas of the Living Building Challenge around the world and in so doing changing it for the better.

CHAPTER 2

Looking Forward to Failure

*Failure isn't fatal, but failure
to change might be.*

— JOHN WOODEN

THE PHRASE "FAILURE IS NOT AN OPTION" has been attributed to Gene Kranz, the lead flight director for Houston-based Mission Control, as he directed NASA personnel on the ground to devise a method of saving the crew aboard the damaged *Apollo 13* spacecraft (shown in Figure 2.1) in 1970. While these five words played great on the big screen when the true tale made its way to Hollywood, and they help to define a dramatic episode in American culture, the real story behind them, I would venture to guess, is far more complicated. In fact, what allowed the ground crew to succeed in this historically tense situation were their many failures that led to that moment. Because without failure—sometimes repeated failures—there can be no context in which to place success. In the end, the crew of *Apollo 13* landed safely despite overwhelming odds.

We are taught in our culture that winners win, and losers lose. It is a fairly black-and-white assessment, and it is repeated often. It is particularly strong in the American (and to a lesser extent Canadian) mythos that we do not accept failure in ourselves or in others. Period.

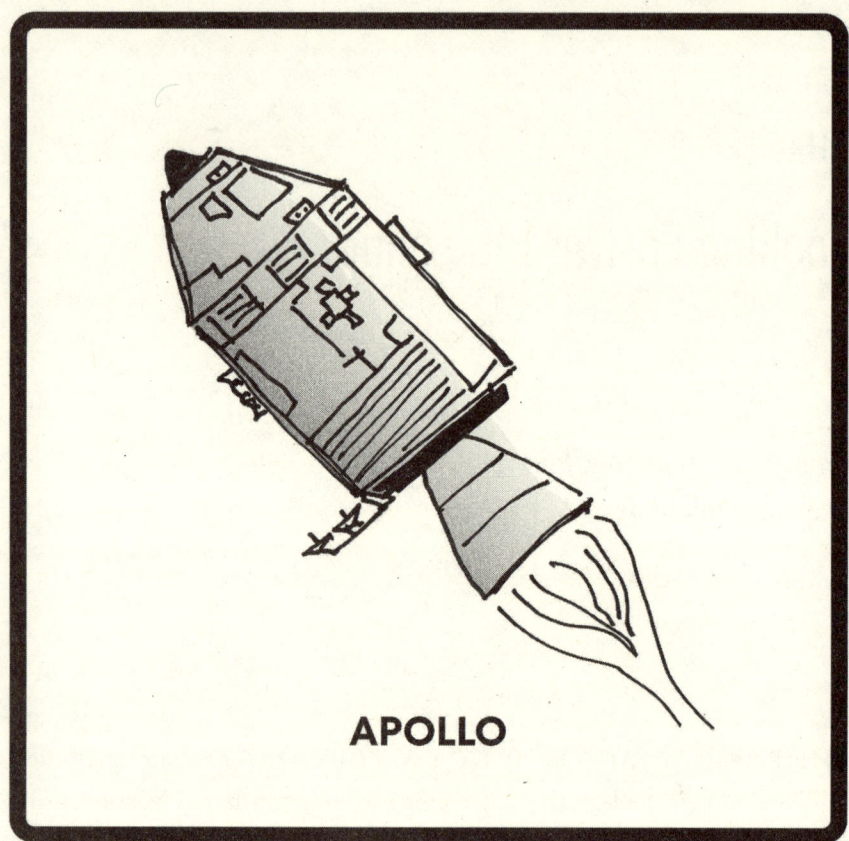

FIGURE 2.1: A sketch of *Apollo 13*—the project where "failure is not an option" was coined.

However, anyone who has ever thought *I will never do/say/eat/build* that *again* knows the wisdom of making mistakes. How would we ever learn how to do things better if we denied ourselves the opportunity to do things badly? In this way, our failures help define us, perhaps even more powerfully than our victories.

Intellectually, this reasoning makes perfect sense. "If at first you don't succeed, try, try again" is repeated for good reason. But most of us still go to great lengths to avoid failure, primarily to protect our egos and our fragile sense of self-worth. Our sense of our own strength is tied to our internal track record of wins and losses. Many people have an inner monologue that is self-critical and at times paralyzing. To people who suffer from this affliction, nothing they do is ever good enough, so they have to revisit their work over and over in the futile hopes that it will keep getting better so they feel better—and ironically they reach a point where the quality of the work actually goes down *because of* their repeated effort.

In addition, we become emotionally attached to our ideas and projects in a way that creates a sense of personal loss when things do not go well or we get negative feedback from others. We wrongly equate our self-worth to the things we do rather than the spirit in which we do them. Thus, our affection for our own work limits our ability to detach from it and allow it to fail, which in turn limits the very potential of the work. When the work we do gets criticized, it feels like we're being criticized personally, and this dynamic reinforces the wrong sets of behaviors.

From a young age, we are taught to take ourselves seriously. We learn that when we succeed with our childhood milestones, at school, in relationships, and in our careers, we are praised and rewarded. Our society focuses on the most polished outcomes, often at the expense of the most innovative or forward-thinking ideas. Substance can take a backseat to style, and style that is superficial gets rewarded.

When one becomes an "expert" in a given subject, they're expected always to possess a certain wealth of information in that area—certainly not to fail! An expert always knows and is not afforded the luxury of ignorance. When we are accustomed to success and taught that failures are "not an option," even small mistakes feel catastrophic. The reality, however, is that our moderate and sometimes large failures lead to our greatest accomplishments.

What is missing in our culture, and in business in general, is our willingness to thrust ourselves out there on that seemingly fragile limb where failure is likely to occur repeatedly. We have lost the ability to be friends with failure, and this loss is very dangerous when you consider the size of the environmental and social obstacles we face. A risk-averse culture usually finds itself on the decline. When a baby takes countless tumbles, testing the limits and discovering the abilities of her physical self as she learns to walk, she is learning from and embracing failure. If we caught her every time she wobbled, she would never succeed independently.

My great personal mentor, an architect named Bob Berkebile, was a student of the transformative thinker Buckminster Fuller in the 1950s. He once observed Fuller point out to the mother of a teetering toddler that allowing the boy to fall was the ideal way to teach him about gravity! Instead, as most parents would do, she swooped in to stop her son from taking a very modest fall. Fuller's point was that a small tumble now would impart an important lesson for later.

As professionals, when we relegate our biggest ideas to the back shelf for fear of failure, we stunt our own development. Holding our work back is often holding ourselves back.

The irony here is that we create a negative feedback loop in which our timidity leads to mediocrity, which can eventually damage our self-esteem and awareness, further limiting our success. In this model, our successes become our failures.

As we head straight into the headwinds of climate change and a radically changing world, we face a time of great transition. Society needs more and more people who are willing to lead and put forward big ideas for social, cultural, and environmental improvement—and who are brave enough to fail by taking intelligent risks. These courageous individuals will have the power to revolutionize civilization. But even when the stakes are much lower—whether you're a student or a small business owner—do not hamper your progress by only playing it safe.

There's no better example of a revolutionary thinker than Buckminster Fuller himself, who was one of the last century's greatest minds. When Bob Berkebile was a student at the University of Kansas in the late 1950s, Fuller served as a guest professor. Fuller's futuristic ideas about architecture and the environment seemed eccentric to some at the time, but his students were enthusiastic about his teachings. In the class Berkebile attended, Fuller incorporated his concept of *tensegrity*, or tensional integrity, which was in its early phases. Fuller asked the students to design a tensegrity structure based on the conceptual guidelines he provided. The group then worked together to build the various members (structural components), which they planned to assemble outside of campus in a much-anticipated public demonstration of the great

Buckminster Fuller's revolutionary design. In a tensegrity structure, once all the components are properly connected and the final tension is applied, they can seemingly pop or spring into their final form through the balanced forces of tension and compression (see Figure 2.2).

The day came, the group gathered, and the audience watched as each student grabbed a piece of the form and slowly stepped backward, allowing the structure to take shape and history to be made. Berkebile and his fellow students were exhilarated to be part of such a momentous event and were proud of the contributions they had made both individually and as a class. With one final step, they provided the last bit of necessary tension and awaited the moment in which the tensegrity dome would

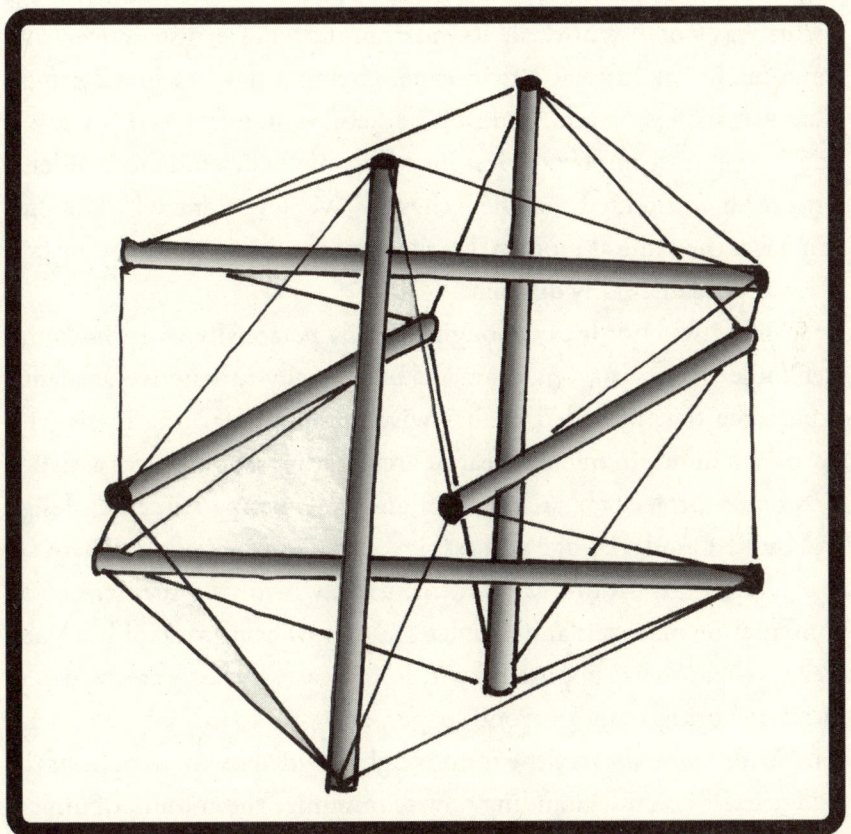

FIGURE 2.2: A tensegrity structure is an almost magical-looking construction whereby nearly every member is in tension and only a few compression members "float" inside it. Tensegrity structures can take different forms.

erect itself. Instead, they watched as one member buckled, the structure collapsed, and the entire project fell apart.

The experiment had failed. Their hard work was for nothing. They were devastated.

"Yes, we've done it!" they heard Fuller exclaim. He gathered his dejected students around the pieces that lay on the ground and enthusiastically praised them for a job well done. He quickly pointed out that they had performed the most crucial experiment of all—they had uncovered the weakness in the structure and in the theory of tensegrity itself. Armed with this new, extremely valuable information, they could now make a bigger and better structure and rely more confidently on its success. They had found Fuller's own error. While the lesson was not intentional, it was infinitely more instructive—and some might say historic—than experiencing a flawless first attempt. That was sixty years ago, and Bob Berkebile still refers to this story as one of the most important lessons of his life. The students suddenly felt proud and puffed out their chests: "We *have* done it!" The outcome was the same as moments earlier, but the spirit of embracing failure was fundamentally different.

While I was not lucky enough to study personally with Buckminster Fuller, I recall a less dramatic but equally instructive academic experience that provided similar wisdom about learning to sit with my own failures. In my first year of architecture school, I was assigned a common project for architecture and engineering students: design and build a model bridge and test it to the point of failure. There are many variations on this assignment, usually involving restrictions on construction materials and stipulations of how heavy and for how long weight needs to be supported by it. In our case, the assignment was to build our bridges out of wood, paper, and cardboard only. The winning bridge would carry the most weight divided by the weight of the bridge itself, so understanding how to minimize the amount of unnecessary material was an important part of the assignment. Efficiency was key. As designers, we naturally wanted our bridges to look attractive as well. Like most students, I wanted my bridge to stand out. Mine would be the strongest, the best-looking, and the most memorable, so I spent a great deal of time working on the design and "perfecting" how my bridge would go together. My partner and I looked at photos, sketched alternatives, calculated weight loads, gathered supplies, and crafted a beautiful span.

As the day approached, we were excited and proud of the amazing structure we had built—our confidence was palpable. Unfortunately, the reality was quite the opposite. When it was our turn, the professor brought out the weights and hooked them up to our bridge. Immediately, the bridge began to sag to one side and then—*bang*—collapsed in a spectacular explosion. It stood out all right—by failing almost immediately! Our only consolation was that we were not alone; many students had made the same mistakes we did. The problem was that we'd all been so busy *designing* our bridges that we'd forgotten to *test* them for the very properties that would ultimately make them fail. We'd been so confident in the design process that we hadn't allowed for the possibility of failure in the construction process, a mistake that eventually led to a much bigger failure: a poor grade on the assignment.

The next year was very different. Learning from my mistakes, I adjusted my strategy accordingly. The key lesson was that I needed to learn from failure. So instead of spending all my time on the design and then hoping for success, I built several bridges and tested them on my own until they failed. Each time, I observed my error and quickly built another. My partner and I switched to cardboard and paper so that we could construct several test bridges in a fraction of the time that it took to build with wood. The day of the competition brought forth a bridge with multiple prototypes behind it. And unlike the year before, pound after pound was added to the bridge, as people looked on with surprise: *A cardboard bridge that strong?* When it did fail, we cheered—knowing that in some small way we had changed our own paradigm of loss, failure, and true success.

The great metaphor at play with this assignment is profound. Every bridge, no matter how well built, always reaches a point where it fails. It's only a question of how long it takes.

In my subsequent career, my failures have led me to my greatest moments.

While I can't say that I love to fail, the lessons learned are never lost on me and I rarely take them to heart in a negative way for long. I've been blessed to have had an amazing and successful career, and people sometimes comment on how much I manage to get done successfully. I usually just grin at them, since what they don't realize is that I actually have a fairly poor "hit rate." It's just that I have swung at a lot of pitches and when I miss, I get right back in the batter's box and adjust my stance or swing while others are still pondering their next move. Eventually, I do hit the ball.

The greatest batting average of all time is only .366 for Ty Cobb, which means that over 60 percent of the time he failed. It's a good lesson to learn in order to calibrate expectations. Yet, the more frequently you get ideas ¾ baked and out into the world, and then learn from your failures, the better your batting average will get as well.

I would like to think that I now make many fewer mistakes than I used to, but I rely on the fact that my many screwups have allowed me to find the path toward my own success. I force myself to be open to professionally vulnerable situations, I refuse to perfect an idea prior to its release, and I fight the urge to retreat in the face of failure. I have found that the rewards are greater when I resist timidity. Put things out into the world, be open to what kind of feedback you get, and keep refining. Each iteration and each time you do something, it will get better and better—and so ¾ baked becomes a moving scale sliding toward greatness.

This is the magic of imperfection at work.

The trick, I believe, is to seek the balance between success and failure—and not to allow ourselves to be overly swayed by either. Our greatest ideas are cultivated in that middle ground between dejection and overconfidence. From there, they take authentic shape, and the universe accepts them most readily. Failure, then, is our most important teacher and has the power to lead us to magical moments. Not only is failure an option, it is a necessity.

¾ BAKED SECRET

Look for opportunities to test yourself.

Be willing to fail, not just once but as many times as necessary, for it's in the failure that true success is found.

To understand why something works, learn how and why it doesn't.

¾ BAKED SECRET

Embrace when something doesn't go as originally planned, and recognize that there is great value in having assumptions and ideas proven wrong.

For true growth, learn how to change rather than doing anything possible to not be wrong.

Remember that only the fool views success as never having been wrong.

Developing an Inner Compass

Think about someone young that you love—perhaps your child, grandchild, or a niece or nephew. When a young child draws something, like a picture of a house, it is likely far from perfect if we're judging it by how realistic it is. Objectively speaking, the drawing might be quite "bad" or rough around the edges. It might not even be clear what it is, but to the child it represents an idea or place or person they feel strongly about.

Hopefully, when presented with such a drawing, you don't belittle it and scold the child for their lack of adherence to reality (although, sadly, that's likely the experience of a lot of youngsters who give up art at an early age). Instead, you might praise the child for their creativity and for their use of color or texture or different elements of creativity they've expressed. You might even hang the drawing on your fridge to show your appreciation for them and your value of their ¾ baked expression.

Further conversations might include teaching the child some drawing techniques and watching over time at how the same drawing evolves and improves as the child gets older. Their external representation of their inner world becomes clearer and more refined precisely because they got appropriate feedback from the world. Children who shut down and are afraid to express themselves rarely get better.

Why is it so different when we consider ourselves as our own audience? Why are we so harsh and self-limiting? Are we merely passing on negative feedback we got as a child, having internalized the critique? We must do better when it comes to our own work.

Just like you wouldn't judge a child you love for the quality of their art, you shouldn't attach your own merit to the quality of something you're working on. You should simply acknowledge what it is—something that needs work, needs feedback, needs help, and yet is a perfectly fine expression of where you are at this time.

If it needs help, ask for help. If it is good enough, then share it with others. The art of the ¾ baked philosophy involves building an internal compass that can review and assess with objectivity and that approaches the process of learning from failure from a place of kindness and personal growth.

The great writer Antoine de Saint-Exupéry, who wrote numerous French classics in the early 20th century, was by all assessments a much less talented illustrator than author, yet that did not stop him. In his masterpiece *The Little Prince*, he included several highly imperfect drawings to convey simple ideas he thought helped his story. Once viewed, his drawing of an elephant inside a boa constrictor is unforgettable. Imperfect or not, the character of the little prince and Saint-Exupéry's crude drawings inspired millions of people and has led to multiple movies, cartoons, new illustrations, and toys since Saint-Exupéry's untimely death during World War II. There was magic in the imperfection he released to the world, and through the imagination of his countless readers, he achieved perfection.

When to Avoid Failure

What are the true consequences of failure? This is a question we should ask ourselves as we begin any important assignment or task. The answer can provide a clear rudder to guide our efforts. If a consequence is life or death—if you're working on a moon landing program, for instance—then it warrants the highest level of your attention and focus.

Yet the consequences most people face are not life and death and are likely much less dramatic. The ¾ baked philosophy is therefore inherently one of calibration. The more that's at stake, the more emphasis there is on perfection, to be sure, but with that emphasis should come the desire to have early mini-failures and to cultivate outside feedback as soon as possible in order to keep tacking toward the best possible outcome.

Before building a rocket that carries people, for instance, you test and build-to-fail rockets that do not carry people, so you can learn where the weak points are without the high-stakes consequences. Acknowledging that the consequences of failure are mostly in our heads and tied up with our emotions and insecurities should free us up to quit worrying so much and just get our work done. Save your stress and need for perfection for when the stakes are really high, and you'll have more reserves and stamina for dealing with them.

CHAPTER 3

The Magic of Feedback

*If you are self-taught, you had a fool
for a teacher.*

— MARK TWAIN

THE ¾ BAKED PHILOSOPHY is not about producing shoddy or incomplete work. Far from it. In fact, as you practice the approach, over time your ¾ baked effort will be as good or better than what others produce, no matter how hard they try or how long they take, because it focuses on continuous improvement. And the difference is feedback.

As we have already discussed, trying to perfect everything on your own is a fool's errand. Our job is to get our ideas and work out in the world using the ideal allocation of effort and timing so that we can let "the universe" help us perfect it without burning ourselves out. The higher the rate of meaningful feedback (through testing what we do), the better we become over time. Knowing when to stop and share, and being open to the results regardless of the outcome, puts us in an incredible position to keep learning and improving. That is why it's essential to find mentorship and peers we can collaborate with. In sports, it is always useful to practice with someone just a little bit better than you; in so doing, you sharpen your skills and pick up new ones. That's why even the world's greatest athletes still have coaches. The same is true in life and business.

The world is full of mentors waiting to share. And there are different kinds—some who can give you blunt feedback, others who can teach you new skills or techniques, and still others who simply inspire you. In publishing, there are different types of editors, for instance. Some editors help with prose and the flow of ideas, and others copyedit and look for consistency and accuracy—very different skill sets, as it turns out, but both highly important. Even very famous and successful writers rely heavily on their editors to make their work better. If Stephen King and Alice Walker are willing to share their work with others to improve it, should you not be open to sharing yours?

I've always been lucky to have had amazing mentors throughout my life—wise elders and smart peers who have helped me become better and better at what I do. But, of course, it's not just luck—I must ask for help and be smart enough to then take it.

I count my parents and family as key early mentors, and I had some great professors in university. Once I started my architecture career, I had the opportunity to learn from some wise and seasoned architects who taught me a great deal in a very short amount of time. But even now, when I am the one with more grey hair than most of my project team members, I surround myself with people who constantly make what I do better and better through feedback. Sometimes mentors can come in a variety of packages.

In my architectural team, for example, I employ professionals with a wide variety of skills, and the key has always been to hire people who are better than I am at certain things. I have graphic designers and visualizers who are better than me at what they do. I have engineers who are more technically accurate, and I have other architects and designers with more experience putting buildings together and the ability to properly detail construction sets. And, of course, I bring skills that they don't have as well—but as a team we constantly share information and feedback and make each other better and stronger. We rely on each other, and we learn together and develop projects together that eventually get built. It is amazing that a handful of people can work together to produce the blueprints for a complex $100 million building, located thousands of miles away from our office, but that's what we do every year. None of us could achieve it by ourselves, but a team of just a few people with the right skills and the right quality control procedures can create something magical on a site where nothing existed before.

¾ BAKED SECRET

Find a mentor, not a hero.

We all walk in the shadows of others, so acknowledge and honor those who have taught you.

To be effective, continually find mentors, partners, and collaborators, which means shedding the mythology of the lone creative genius.

Recognize and acknowledge that almost everyone has something to teach, but mentors must be approachable and willing to teach and share their knowledge and expertise.

Remember that mentors don't have to be "stars"; all they need to know is something you don't or how to do things in ways you currently aren't.

Be humble and learn; resist the notion that you're an "expert" with nothing else to learn.

Seeking Out Critical Feedback

One way that architects move their work toward better and better outcomes is to pin up their work and elicit feedback from their team. In architectural jargon, this is known as a *crit*, and it's an intense and sometimes vulnerable practice wherein you share your ideas and design work at various stages of completion in order for others to provide feedback—sometimes quite critically.

In architecture schools, the crit is one of the fundamental ways that designers learn. Students will pin up their work and typically get a brief amount of time to present it; and then a group of critics—typically more seasoned architects and professors and sometimes peers—proceed to tell them what's wrong with it or what's working well. It concentrates the time and type of feedback deemed to be most helpful for students to further develop their work. By pinning everything up on a large wall—or digitally on a "miro" or shared electronic board, others can see the totality of the student's effort and their work can be judged on its merits alone.

At some architecture schools, the process can be quite brutal. When I studied at the Mackintosh School of Architecture (part of the Glasgow School of Art) in the mid-nineties, the professors seemed to take perverse delight in tearing down their students' work—ostensibly competing for who could get in the more clever and insightful barb and elicit laughter from the crowd gathered around to watch. It definitely helped thicken your skin! The point, of course, was that you needed to develop a level of detachment from your ideas so that you could critically evaluate them, and not merely fall in love with what you did because you created it—or get discouraged. We often treat our work as too precious and, because we are attached to it in unhealthy ways, resist changes. When we hear feedback on something we've done, we take it personally and get defensive, feel hurt, or shut down. When we do that, our growth stops. We can't internalize how to improve something on its own terms, as it's somehow wrapped up in our own insecurities and ego needs. We feel personally judged and we attach our self-worth to what we created. None of these reactions serves the goal of creating effective change. Our ego is holding on too tightly to our work.

Remember, you are not your work! Getting comfortable with accepting feedback also teaches you when it is appropriate to push back and defend what you have done, because you objectively understand both its weaknesses and its strengths.

It's essential to calibrate an inner critic that is not your ego in disguise. When you can do that, you become a better judge of your own strengths and limits and can then work to better yourself effectively. You begin to expand your ability to see different perspectives and learn to solve problems in numerous ways, not just "our way." Other professions would be wise to take a page from the training that architects go through in this regard.

The Power of the Parti

Perfection is achieved when there is nothing left to take away.

—ANTOINE DE SAINT-EXUPÉRY

What do architects look for in their work? What is it that separates mere building from architecture? Well, many things do, but one element that is critically important is the clarity of the architectural idea expressed in the building. Architects look for a clear diagram or organizational framework that can help them organize the many complex components within a building—its circulation, structure, and mechanical systems, for instance. Doing so makes a building more legible and less confusing. Architects call this a *parti diagram*.

A good building can be quickly described by a simple sketch, or *parti*, that conveys the essence of how it is organized. This use of the word *parti* originates from architectural training in the 19th century at the famous École des Beaux-Arts in Paris and was a way of ensuring that the main idea of the design was continually strengthened as a building design developed over time. Design elements that diluted or confused the parti were considered critically. The point is to refine, simplify, and strengthen the main ideas as much as possible. In other words, the parti is a tool intended to enforce rigor, ensure simplicity, and create clarity in the work. The great 20th century architect Ludwig Mies van der Rohe famously declared "less is more" as a statement of virtue in design. Subtraction, not addition, resulted in greater architectural purity.

These are ideas that can translate to many fields and many assignments. What is the "big idea" for your work? What are you trying to convey? Is it clear to others? Does everything in the work make the big idea stronger and clearer? Are you trying to do too much? Are you, in fact, unclear on what your big idea even is?

Solving for essence is what I call the work of making anything we do no more complicated than it has to be to get the job done. It's part of a philosophical approach of ¾ baked whereby we aim for simplicity over complexity. Keep removing layers or unnecessary steps or elements, and do the essential things really well. This approach is just as helpful for writers working on reports or anything creative as for architects designing buildings. It is also a great mantra for the making of any physical thing; a new widget of any kind benefits from the approach of solving for essence. A simple menu at most restaurants is better than a complex one, and a clear set of instructions at a hospital or assembly line ensures fewer mistakes and better outcomes. It's all about editing and refinement.

A fun example comes from the history of beer making in Germany. In the 15th century, Bavaria passed beer purity laws, or *Reinheitsgebot*. These regulations stated that only four ingredients could be used to make beer: water, barley, hops, and yeast. Anything else was considered extraneous and diminished the essence of what beer should be. At the time, political and resource reasons were behind the restrictions, but despite these seeming limitations brewers were able to make some extraordinary and highly varied beers.

As a thought exercise, consider how few components, elements, or words you could use to do any job or project required in your work.

Asking for Help

Why did some of us become conditioned to avoid asking for help? I believe our society teaches us many bad lessons, including that it's a sign of weakness to ask for or need help, exemplified by the associated myth of the "lone genius" who does everything without assistance. In fact, it should be the most natural thing in the world to ask for help since we are a social species that only survives and thrives together. I often see people at work who keep struggling at something when they could simply ask for help and complete it sooner and better.

In team sports, you learn quickly that you need your other team members to win. In theory, at work it should be the same thing, where everyone in a given company or organization is on the same team; not asking for help from a coworker who could make your work better is actually wasting your company's resources and everyone's time. You have an obligation, I'd argue, to ask for help whenever you need it or feel bogged down.

Asking for help is in fact the best way in the world to get better at something. This doesn't mean having someone do your work for you, but rather having them help you, mentor you, and show and teach you better ways of solving problems. And it can build very valuable camaraderie and trust. We're so afraid for others to find out that we don't know something, we forget that it's likely apparent anyway in the quality of the work we do. Why are our egos so fragile? Lots of people love to give help and are happy to do so if asked. It's like Mr. Rogers said: "Look for the helpers." They're all around—and you should be one too!

But what if you don't like getting feedback and prefer to figure it out on your own? I'd argue that this is a self-limiting view. You don't always have to like doing the things that you should do. In service to your work and so you have more time for other things personally and professionally, you should ask for help or feedback whenever you feel stuck or bogged down. What a waste of time otherwise! The irony is that learning from others makes you better—so that over time you do in fact need less help.

Good leaders and talented CEOs that I work with still ask people for help. Too many others fall into the trap of the "expert" who doesn't feel like they can ask for help because they're the ones who should already know the answers. Being afraid to look bad has stopped true greatness in many.

Solving for Essence and Team Size

Too many cooks spoil the broth.

— PROVERB ATTRIBUTED TO
GEORGE GASCOIGNE, 1575

I often get asked, "What is the ideal team size to work on a project?" My answer is a bit cheeky: "No larger than absolutely necessary and no smaller than needed." The prevailing, politically correct thinking is that to produce something good and to be "inclusive," you need to widen the circle as much as possible and include people with diverse backgrounds and viewpoints to create it.

I disagree.

Few great things are *created* by committee or large groups of people. But anything great *and* influential is eventually *refined* by them.

Remember, regardless of how "inclusive" you hope to be with something you are developing, by definition, forming any kind of group means excluding others from it. It is insulting even to think that whole populations can be represented by one member of their group!

Expanding a group too broadly at the outset of an initiative serves only to complicate progress and likely water down the parti or main idea, due to competing visions or understandings of the problem to be solved. The ¾ baked philosophy takes a very different approach that I think is much more authentic in its inclusivity while being dramatically more effective strategically.

The approach again is to develop an idea to a ¾ baked point in time with as few authors as possible, as efficiently as possible. This could be one person or a core team of a half dozen (as long as the members represent a range of expertise for said enterprise) putting the idea out into the world as broadly as practicable for feedback *before* final refinement and adoption. When you take the time to make something as clear as possible, as simple as possible, and get it out into the world, the idea can be evaluated on its own terms efficiently and effectively. Bad ideas will come to light quickly and good ideas will be made better by those reviewing them, and often the best feedback comes from people you may have considered unlikely contributors. (See Figure 3.1.)

The problems I see on many projects often stem from either

- things going to market without enough testing and feedback, or

- ideas that are the product of "groupthink," with too many contributors who believe they are representing viewpoints as proxies and that serve only to complicate the work.

An engaging article by Brett Lovelady in *Fast Company* called "Design Is a Point of View: Seven Truths in Designing" supports my thesis regarding team size:

> Design is not a democracy. Democracies are fine, mainly for collecting diverse input. But they can kill design. Often too many opinions water down the clarity of the design intent. I've had many clients where there are way too many brilliant people involved in programs. They find it their duty to provide all the alternative solutions or insights to every program—always broadening the thinking instead of focusing on decision-making. If not for the benevolent dictatorship of the program director in these programs, they would never reach the goal. Design requires focused leadership, not democratic consensus.[1]

¾ BAKED SECRET

Solve for essence—distill your work down to its simplest version.

Make sure ideas are clearly understood and conveyed with clarity.

Start small but quickly expand circles of feedback.

Refine and repeat.

Work with as small a team as possible to get clarity around an idea, then broaden liberally and solicit feedback widely—not the other way around.

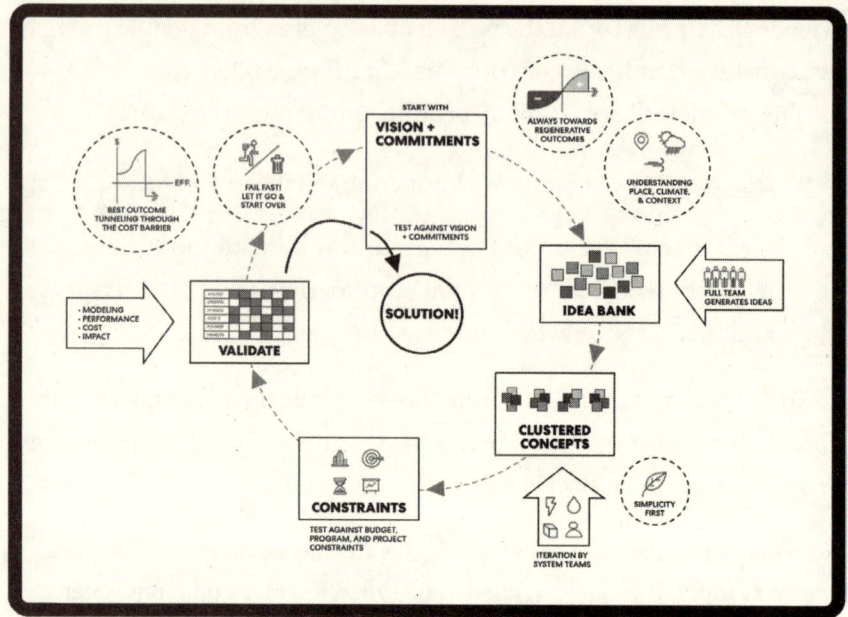

FIGURE 3.1: The "integrated design process" my team at McLennan Design uses to design green buildings. Notice that we start with vision, brainstorm quickly, test, and refine with a willingness to "fail fast." (Source: McLennan Design.)

The Honest Voice Within

One of the magically imperfect results of the ¾ baked approach is the cultivation of an *honest* inner voice that can more objectively provide much of its own feedback. As you learn to exchange feedback more regularly and truly detach yourself from your work with less internal bias, you can train yourself to more quickly and honestly tell when your own ideas are strong or weak. It should never completely replace external feedback, but a dialed-in, inner compass is a great partner to it in the spirit of continuous improvement. The honest voice within is what allows you to hear and incorporate external feedback of any kind and to know when to push back—as not all feedback is helpful or correct! Knowing what feedback to accept or reject is itself a critical skill. This is a powerful idea we'll come back to later in the book that is key to the magic of imperfection.

CHAPTER 4

Calibration and the ¾ Baked Way

*The only calibration that counts is how much
heart people invest, how much they ignore
their fears of being hurt or caught out or
humiliated. And the only thing people regret
is that they didn't live boldly enough, that they
didn't invest enough heart, didn't love enough.
Nothing else really counts at all.*

— TED HUGHES

YOU'RE NOW LIKELY WONDERING, *How do I tell when my work is ¾
baked?* Let's unpack that question together.

We've all seen meat thermometers that are designed to tell us how
long we need to cook various proteins so that they're safe to eat (see
Figure 4.1). Some meat, like chicken, can carry tough-to-kill organisms
like salmonella and must be cooked to at least 165 degrees throughout to
be safe, whereas steak only needs to get to 145 degrees to be declared safe
by the USDA. Many people cook their beef even rarer with good outcomes because the most troublesome bacteria found in red meat is often
only surface borne (which is why you can have beef with a pink center).
Meat thermometers provide another helpful metaphor about applying

the right effort to the context at hand. In a sense, these simple tools tell us how much effort or energy needs to be expended before the "product" can be consumed. Knowing the difference between cooked and under-cooked can be a big deal for our well-being.

We should think of our work like this too. Not everything is equal in importance, and the ramifications or symptoms of "undercooking" an idea can vary from none at all to life threatening. If you cook a steak too long, it becomes tough and lifeless, and even the best cuts of meat lose their character, but ultimately it's no big deal. Yet cooking a chicken too little—well, that could kill you or at least really make you suffer for a couple of days!

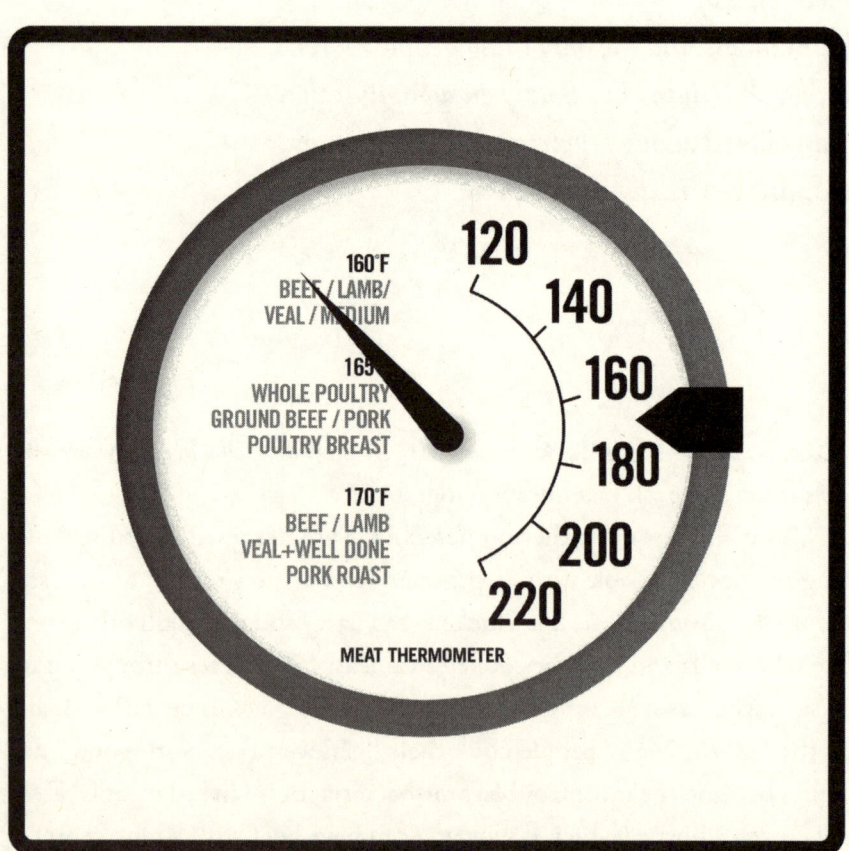

FIGURE 4.1: A good meat thermometer helps ensure food safety.

Developing our inner compass or gauge is therefore essential in the ¾ baked philosophy, allowing us to better use our time and save our energy for when things really matter. What this metaphor also reveals is that the definition of when something is fully baked, half-baked, or ¾ baked **changes dramatically based on the assignment and context.**

You might admire coworkers or colleagues who give every assignment "their all" regardless of its importance, but I think those individuals likely have an unhealthy relationship with their work. They are often the same people who never seem to have time for their families or friends or who make unnecessary and irrelevant sacrifices for little real benefit. Rather than psychoanalyzing them, let's look to learn another way.

The Significance Meter

The first step in building our internal effort gauge is to put things in proper perspective. As we start any task, we should reflect on its importance and its gravity based on its potential success or failure.

A seven-point scale like the significance meter in Figure 4.2 might be useful.

You are obviously free to adjust the scale or naming convention as you see fit, but the key step here is to quickly assess the importance and consequences of the deliverable and calibrate your efforts accordingly. A ¾ baked effort for a critically important deadline that could cost you your job is very different from one where the task is of minor importance or someone simply needs feedback on a rough draft. When there are so many things in life to focus on, a one-size-fits-all approach to effort is foolish, wasteful, or—if the task and effort are gauged and scaled improperly—even dangerous and foolhardy.

We spend too much of our time and energy on things of little consequence, and we perversely procrastinate or give insufficient attention to those that really matter. Why? Often it's simply because we don't take the time to think about it or we prioritize what's fun or enjoyable or easiest rather than what's essential. For tasks of low importance, we often should question whether they're even worth doing at all! Calibrating your internal meter is helpful in learning to say no to anything not worth doing.

As you do this calibrating exercise going forward, you should ask yourself about anything in the last two categories: *Should I even be doing this? Why am I doing it?* And, if you decide to do it, take the pressure off since you've already acknowledged that the consequences are trivial. Have fun with it and get it done efficiently! As the saying goes, don't sweat the small stuff.

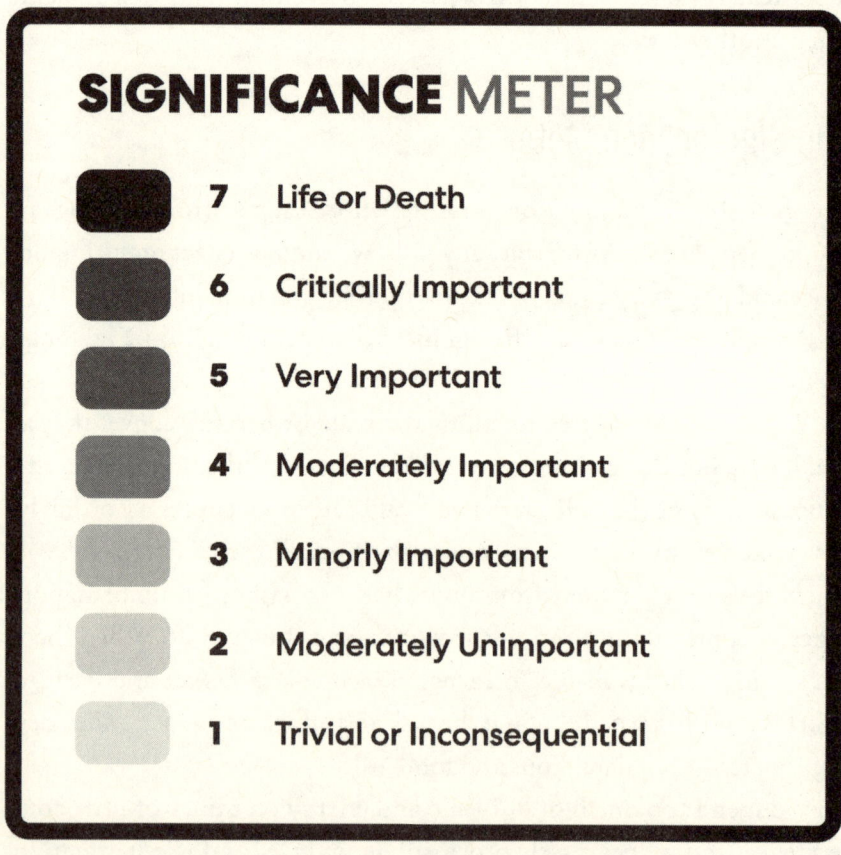

FIGURE 4.2: The significance meter helps you assess how important the things you're working on are.

¾ BAKED SECRET

Not everything is of equal importance—so don't treat everything the same.

Say no to things that don't need to be done.

Work harder on the things that really matter.

Calibrate your efforts to consequences.

Do the important things first!

The Joy/Satisfaction Meter

Eliminating whole tasks or matching the efforts we expend on them to their importance is generally a smart strategy in time management, but there are exceptions, of course. The first is that while something might be unimportant to you, it might be very important to your boss or your client or your spouse. The ¾ baked philosophy is not an excuse to be lazy, nor is it an excuse to be callous or uncaring. Sometimes we do things for others regardless of a task's importance to us personally, because we care about our relationships. In this way, something might start out as unimportant but become more important when you account for others' feelings or objectives.

Also be careful not to assume things in this regard. If you're doing something for someone else, do they in fact think it is as important as you do? Do they even want you to do it? Double-checking with the other person about how they rate a task's relevance and importance is essential to ensure alignment. Using the significance meter as a communication tool is a good idea. Too often, I've seen people focusing on things they thought would help someone when that help wasn't even desired—what a waste!

Thinking about the relevance of any task should also spark you to question your own agency with the task at hand: *Am I the best one to do this task? Do I need help? Should someone else be doing some or all of it?* It might be that the task is better delegated or shared with others.

One more point to acknowledge: sometimes we do things not because they are important or have consequences, but simply because they bring us joy or satisfaction. Spending time to recharge your batteries is essential, and making time for family, friends, and yourself is an underlying motivation of the ¾ baked philosophy. If you properly scale your efforts with everything you do, it follows that you'll have more time available for things you value in your life, including spending time on seemingly frivolous yet joyous activities! The joy/satisfaction meter (Figure 4.3) is another helpful tool to think about how you might classify the things you are working on.

JOY | SATISFACTION METER

7   Lifelong Dream Fulfillment

6   Extremely Fun & Rewarding Activity

5   Fun Rewarding Activity

4   Mildly Rewarding Activity

3   Benign Activity

2   Unpleasant Activity

1   Dreaded Activity

FIGURE 4.3: The joy/satisfaction meter helps you assess how much joy or personal satisfaction you derive from the things you're working on.

¾ BAKED SECRET

Value your time—it's one of the most important resources you have.

Save your energy for the things that matter and apply more of your efforts to those rather than less important activities.

Consider not doing tasks of little importance or consequence unless they serve a greater purpose or help maintain important relationships.

Don't sweat the small stuff.

Order-of-Operations Thinking

In grade-school math class, you probably learned about the order of operations, a sequence you had to follow to get the right answer when solving an equation. You might remember it as PEMDAS: parentheses, exponents, multiplication and division from left to right, and addition and subtraction from left to right. Here's a simple example of applying PEMDAS to get different answers to equations that use the same numbers:

$$(5 + 3) \times 2 = 16$$
$$5 + (3 \times 2) = 11$$

The rank of the operation, known as its *precedence*, is another great metaphor for getting stuff done in our lives. When you have a list of ten things to do, take a minute and rank them! Give them a precedence order. Then, just like when solving a math equation, work on the more important things *first* if you can, or at least prioritize them over less important items.

Then, you might get quick things out of the way; consider which tasks you need to do to avoid slowing down others who are trying to get their work done. Too often, people prioritize what's easy or convenient even when they know the consequences of leaving the most important stuff for last.

Temporal Calibration

After gauging the relative importance of anything you're working on, you need to insert a time dimension to it. In the next chapter, I'll discuss how every task should have a deadline, but going beyond that aspect, you should always assess up front how much time and energy completing the task will take. Some projects are quite quick, and some can take months, and this timeframe must play a role in your planning efforts. Building on the idea of the seven-point significance meter, you can add a time dimension from tasks that can be done quickly to those that will take months to complete.

You can then plot both scales on a four-square graph with time on the horizontal axis and importance on the vertical, as shown in Figure 4.4.

This simple tool allows you to see the field of activity you're working on through a multidimensional lens.

Things in the upper-left quadrant have quick turnaround times and are ranked important to critical in their consequences. You should prioritize anything in this quadrant above other tasks, and give it the most carefully calibrated ¾ baked effort so that you can meet your deadlines after you've given others a chance to help you fully bake it.

Tasks in the upper-right quadrant are also highly important but have a longer burn. You need to plan for them so that you're not constantly putting them off, and calibrate your efforts accordingly. You'll likely be getting other tasks done while continuing this work, so it's a matter of pacing and keeping momentum. Don't wait to plan for these tasks until later; long-range deadlines should still elicit upfront thinking. Plan the work up front (remember your mise en place) so that you can do the work at a reasonable pace.

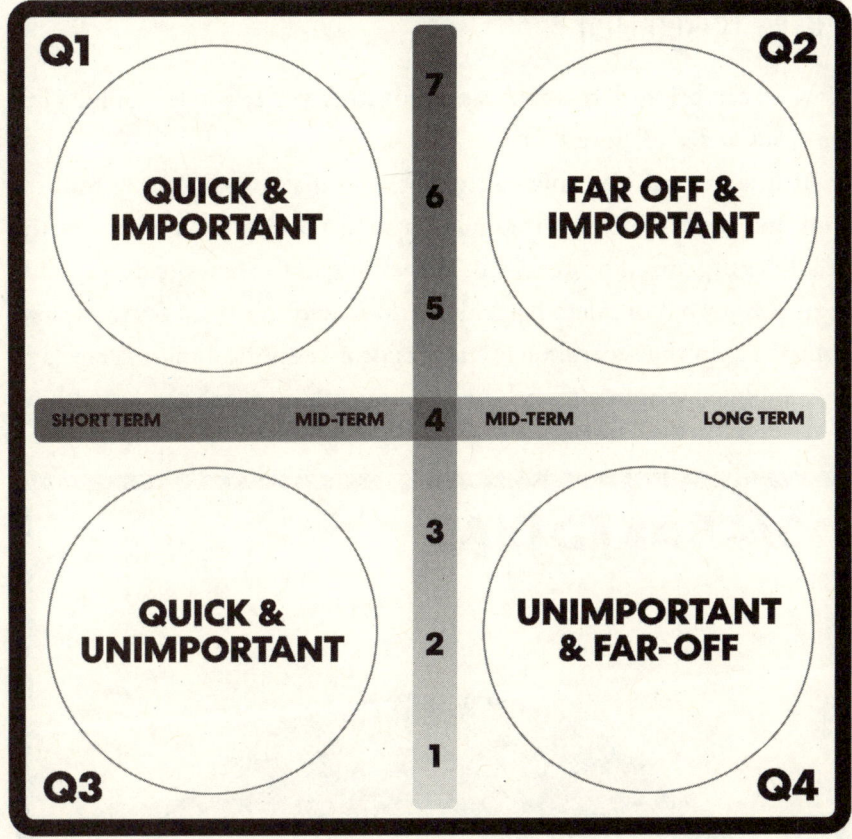

Q = QUADRANT

FIGURE 4.4: How you approach any task should depend on which quadrant of importance it falls in.

Tasks in the lower-right quadrant are of less importance and will take a great deal of time or are far off. These are activities you should really question. Should you even work on them? If yes, why? Can you plan to give this work less effort or delegate it?

Things in the lower-left quadrant are quick and unimportant; you might still do them precisely *because* they take less effort, or perhaps to build goodwill or get practice. However, you should never work on these items at the expense of those in the upper two quadrants. At any given time, you should do a little bit of this type of work, but never give it too much effort.

The ¾ Baked Dial

Now we can bring all this calibration together with a single graphic I call *the ¾ baked dial* (Figure 4.5).

If it is helpful, use this concentric ring dial as a planning tool for your own workflow. In this graphic, you can see the immediacy of the deadlines organized by quadrant. Something in the first quadrant is due soon or must be completed quickly, perhaps within a week or two or less. Something in the second quadrant has near-term deadlines; it needs to be completed within a month but no longer than a quarter. Something

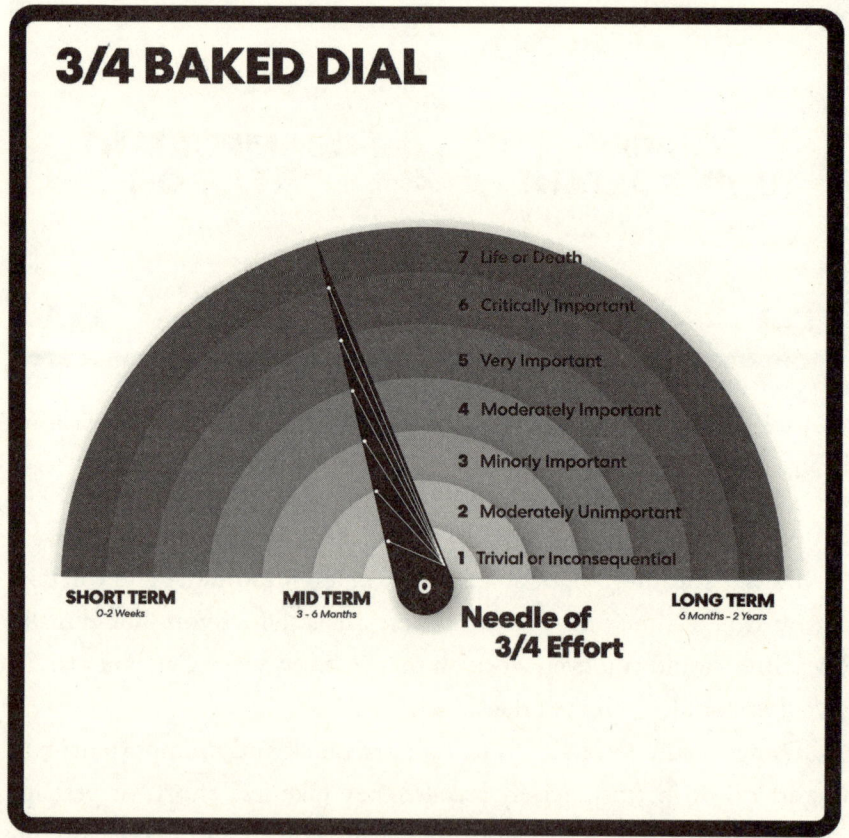

FIGURE 4.5: Use the ¾ baked dial to help think through how important something is, how much effort it will take, and therefore how to calibrate your work to the ¾ baked moment. Note that the needle suggests that the level of effort to reach a ¾ baked moment grows as the importance of the work grows.

in the third quadrant is for longer-term tasks, beyond a quarter and per-haps up to a year. And finally, something in the last quadrant is very long-term—longer than a year. This placement process isn't an exact science; you can calibrate according to your needs and the nature of your work.

The concentric rings describe the importance of the work in ques-tion—from low importance near the center to great importance at the outer ring. And finally, the ¾ baked calibration ring can move around to communicate the level of effort required. As you can see, a ¾ baked effort for a low-importance idea is a much smaller amount of effort than one for something that is very important.

Do I really use this tool when planning all my work? Well, no, because this is a practice I internalized a long time ago. Once you've done this process a few times, it should become obvious and you'll follow this philosophy naturally without needing to be so explicit about it. But from time to time, when I'm unusually busy with multiple competing dead-lines, I do find that it's useful to test my assumptions using something like this tool.

The dial is also a useful tool for team communication and goal setting as well as to illustrate the ¾ baked approach and set group goals when appropriate. If you have trouble getting things done or have people on your teams who do, you might find it a helpful prop at the very least.

¾ BAKED SECRET

Take the time to organize your work by priority and develop an "order of operations" for the work.

Think strategically about the time dimension—when things are due and how long they take to complete.

Calibrate your efforts and ¾ baked output based on this assessment.

Use the dial to ask key questions:

- Can the work be done in the time required with the resources available?

- If not, what would have to change for that to happen?

- Does the work require too much effort for the value of the assignment?

- Should the work be done at all or by someone else?

- How should other assignments be prioritized based on the order of importance?

See the Discussion Guide in the back of the book for more thoughtful ways to engage these ideas and tools.

CHAPTER 5

The Magic of the Deadline

JUST DO IT.

— NIKE SLOGAN

I'M GOING TO PUT IT OUT THERE: nearly anything worth doing in life should have a deadline. When you start an assignment—no matter what it is—set or ask for a deadline to have it completed. Pencil it in your calendar and then plan how you'll get it done on time or earlier. Plan for some contingencies just to be safe; evaluate how they may affect the progress of the assignment; and, if necessary, adjust your deadline at the outset if you think it's not realistic.

Once you set a deadline, you should treat it as a contract. A contract with yourself, certainly, but if your work affects others (and most things do), your deadline should also be considered a contract with them. When you consistently get things done when you say you will, it has several critical results:

- It helps you to further calibrate how long it takes you to complete tasks so that you can plan more effectively in the future.

- Once you get something done on time, it means you are free to get something else done after that or you have time for non-work activities.

- It diminishes the chance that you'll miss other deadlines or cause other people to miss their deadlines waiting for you to complete something, maintaining the workflow.

- Your coworkers will feel that you're dependable and trustworthy, thus building trust and culture because they can count on you. This should not be taken lightly! By being on time, you honor their time.

- It instills self-confidence and a sense of pride, as you know that you're someone who follows through and delivers.

The deadline is king—and it's central to the ¾ baked philosophy.

Remember, by definition, ¾ baked doesn't mean that the work is perfect by the deadline, but that you've reached the point where it's finished enough to be shared with the world for feedback and to clearly communicate your intention.

Too many people go about their tasks and assignments every day without clear deadlines. Without a due date, how do you know if you're working fast enough and not overthinking the assignment, or if you're on track for success or failure?

If others waiting on your work don't know when you'll be finished with your part, how can they plan for theirs? Not meeting deadlines is often proxy for laziness or at least bad planning—and, in a team setting where it affects others, it's selfish. If you don't make your deadline that someone else is counting on, you're essentially saying that their time is less valuable than yours and they should rearrange their schedule to account for your poor planning and efforts. Nobody wants someone on their team who consistently misses deadlines. At the outset of any assignment, it's wise to share the deadline with anyone who is affected by or counting on your work. Good communication goes a long way, and is essential to a professional approach.

If the tables are turned and you're waiting on others to complete something for you, be as clear as possible about your expectations for the work product—and its deadline!

Insist On a Deadline

People early in their career often say, "Well, my boss didn't give me a deadline, so I didn't know when it was due." That's a poor excuse. As soon as you accept any assignment or task, once you understand *what* it is, your next question should be *when* it's due. If there's no one to tell you that, set your own deadline immediately. I would go a step further and say that whenever you accept a task, you now "own" its deadline; even if you don't know what it is, **it has one.**

Now, you might say, " I don't need a deadline, what I'm working on is just for me." For example, you might be working on a novel or a painting that you never plan on sharing. Nevertheless, I believe that you should set a deadline. Decide what you're going to try to do and set appointments and timeframes. What harm does it do? None. But the good it can do is immense, as it builds discipline, even for creative acts. Setting aside time to paint consistently is good for the painter. Setting aside time to write every day is good for the writer, and exercising every day is good for everyone. Whatever we do, regardless of the stakes, is made better with accountability and a sense of completion.

It is true that sometimes deadlines need to be renegotiated or changed. Shit happens, right? Other things come up and new information emerges. Not being rigid is also a hallmark of the ¾ baked philosophy. If a deadline needs to change, then it gets adjusted and reset—not merely thrown out.

When do you reset a deadline? **As soon as you know you can't get the task done on time** or realize it's not likely. And when do you tell others who will be affected? **Immediately**. It's amazing how often people wait until right before or after an original deadline to let people know they can't meet it. That is irresponsible and the opposite of ¾ baked thinking.

When you need to shift a deadline, telling those who are affected by your work may even prompt them to help you get back on track. At a minimum, it will allow them to adjust their own schedules as early as possible for the least mutual disruption. Not making a deadline from time to time, for good reasons, is human. Not communicating it to your boss, client, or collaborators until late in the game is disrespectful and narcissistic.

There is great power in planning and in doing things in a timely fashion. Think about the difference in the experience of taking a train in North America versus taking one in Switzerland or Japan—places where trains run on time and to the minute. People can plan with confidence and societal stress is greatly reduced. You know you can make your doctor's appointment. You know you won't be late for work. You know you can pick up your children at daycare on time. You can count on things.

Compare that to public transportation in many other places, where people are never exactly certain when buses, trains, or ferries will arrive or depart. When things run erratically, people's daily routines may be significantly compromised. They might be required to make sacrifices such as catching an earlier bus or ferry, or they may accept that they'll be late and leave those that count on them in a state of uncertainty.

Being on time is a form of generosity. To others, and even to yourself.

Procrastination can be a productivity killer for a lot of talented, creative people who are hampered by their own delayed decisions and actions necessary for their work. An antidote for those postponing tendencies, in part, is the act of writing down and committing to a deadline. Even little things can benefit from this discipline. Every night I write down a quick list (it takes two minutes) of everything I'm going to get done the following day. When I can, I assign each task a timeslot. Even activities like "get lunch" or "go for a walk" are on my list so that things important to my mental health and well-being are planned for, built into my daily schedule, and not short-changed.

And then the next day, I religiously cross things off as I complete them—even the "get lunch" line item! This might sound persnickety, but it isn't. Each day, I'm building up my internal compass of what I can accomplish and in what timeframe. It makes my planning more realistic and accurate based on my ability to complete tasks when I say I will. And crossing stuff off a list just plain feels good! Sometimes I look back and I'm astounded by how much I get done in a single day or week while others are still dithering.

It's a good feeling.

¾ BAKED SECRET

Set deadlines to help ensure tasks get done; everything deserves a deadline.

Remember that meeting deadlines is a sign of respect to others and yourself and shows that you value time.

When deadlines need to move, communicate it early so that others can adapt.

Create lists or other tools to track work to be completed.

All we have in this world is our time—meaningful time with loved ones and ourselves and for making the world a better place. So, shouldn't time be given attention? Getting things done that have to get done, if planned right, means more time for the things you love and care about. And that's worth creating a list.

The Power of No

It has to be said that the quickest way to complete a deadline is to not accept an assignment or task in the first place. There is great power in understanding which work or tasks you should take on and which ones you shouldn't. This is less about not doing things you don't want to (we all have to do things we don't want to in business as in life) and more about recognizing when to let others do a task they're better suited for, when to delegate (when you're a manager or leader), and when to question the entire premise of doing something.

More discernment in what we take on is critical in the ¾ baked philosophy. Working on the wrong things generally only leads to half-baked solutions anyway and, worse, steals time and energy away from things that are more important or mission critical. Perfectionists in particular have a habit of taking on things they shouldn't, because they feel they can't trust others to do a good enough job.

Many leaders avoid mentoring or teaching others because it takes more time than simply doing the work themselves—how unfortunate is that?! This is another example of how being caught in the trap of perfectionism can stifle innovation. Such short-term thinking deprives others of the necessary step of learning, failing, and getting better through feedback. The right investment in mentoring frees up more and more time and greatly increases productivity in the long term.

Part of the magic of imperfection is **accepting the imperfections in how others do things,** giving them feedback so they get better, and watching a whole team flourish under the philosophy!

For any task that comes up, take the time to consider if the work

- is really necessary and should even be done,

- could be done better or more efficiently by others, or

- provides an opportunity for mentorship or growth by allowing others to do it instead of you.

Doing this provides a future outlet to enhance productivity but requires accepting ¾ baked contributions by others!

At my architectural studio, McLennan Design, over the years I've assembled a very talented group of individuals with a wide array of skills and diverse backgrounds who are able to jump on a large variety of tasks. Having such a strong team enables me to delegate early and often, and my job is often more as a conductor—providing consistent quality oversight and mentorship when needed. While there are many times where it would be quicker and easier to simply do certain tasks myself, I often resist the urge. Having worked together time and time again on design assignments, we've developed a rhythm or cadence that allows for efficient progress. I push my team to "share early and often" for rapid feedback and constant improvement, which also gives them more frequent touchpoints for mentorship. It has made us into a highly effective,

world-class studio—and inevitably the people who thrive and get pro-
moted are those who have embraced the magic of imperfection themselves and seen their effectiveness and productivity rise by using the ¾
baked secret. Hold on to your work too long, miss deadlines, and don't
learn to calibrate to the effort at hand, and you don't thrive.

Opportunities flow to those who keep the flow going and who, by
embracing feedback, keep getting better and better as the years go on.

CHAPTER 6

The Magic of Momentum

This too shall pass.

—PERSIAN ADAGE

AS A LIFELONG TENNIS PLAYER, I've noticed just how much the game of tennis is one of momentum. Watch enough matches with the pros, and you realize this holds true up to the highest level of the game. Winners are often decided by who can maintain momentum the longest and who can learn to capitalize on the ebbs and flows common in the game. When a good player has momentum, they learn to press their advantage and put even more pressure on their opponent—especially if the other player appears to be struggling with their momentum. Less skilled players ease off.

For some players, momentum is a fleeting thing to enjoy when you have it, when things seem to just go your way. While it's not a tide you can avoid, it is one you can ride for longer stretches if you know how to understand it and utilize it. Your opponent is also battling their own timing of momentum gain and loss, and being situationally aware will help you affect theirs when you can.

It's also helpful to know that when your momentum is down, at some point the tide will turn. Good tennis players also use this knowledge to their advantage. When they see that their opponent has momentum, they try to break it up: they take a bathroom break, they call for a trainer, they stretch out the time between points. Anything to do to break momentum and turn the shift back to themselves. You often see this play out at Wimbledon after rain breaks. A player who was on fire before rain stopped a match comes back and struggles to regain the form they had prior to the break. Shit happens, but momentum is real. We can't ever completely control when momentum shifts due to externalities, but we can dampen its effects and harness the change.

This is just as true in life and business as it is in tennis and other sports. It is certainly true of writing and doing creative works—sometimes you "feel it" and sometimes you don't. Tied into the ¾ baked philosophy is knowing when to stop and when to push hard, and a big part of that is learning to read momentum and to use it to get things done.

When British Royal Navy captain George Vancouver and his crew first met with the Coast Salish tribes in the Pacific Northwest in the 1790s, the two groups often misunderstood each other's motivations and intentions, so different were their cultures and how they thought about things. Arrogance and racism likely played into interpretations, such that the British often assumed the worst of their new trading partners. For example, they were frustrated many times when trading, observing that the Coast Salish interspersed periods of paddling activity with periods where they barely seemed to paddle at all or simply waited in their canoes. The British assumed the Coast Salish were lazy. But in fact, given their detailed knowledge of the tides and currents in their own backyard, including back eddies and countercurrents seemingly not aligned with the day's main ebbs and rises, the Coast Salish were often merely waiting for the optimum moment when the current would push them for most of their journey, getting them to their destination faster and with much less effort. The concept of working smarter, not harder, wasn't lost on them.

Doubling your speed with half the effort is the art of riding momentum. Sometimes you still have to paddle hard to reach a certain point at a certain time, but that's only in service to the longer journey and the total effort expended. This is an apt metaphor for a lot of things.

Life ebbs and flows, and likewise our energy and our creativity come in waves that you can ride or fight. It's essential to learn when to paddle strategically upcurrent and when to wait for an ebb tide to carry you quicker to completion.

Whether you're someone working in business or a student, it is wise to learn the currents and flow of momentum in your life and those of your team. It is critical to understand how inertia can either help you get something done or merely contribute to burnout and stagnation. We all can remember times when our work felt effortless, fun, and easy, as well as times when every task felt like a slog. But we often fail to observe this phenomenon and change our patterns accordingly. Too many initiatives start and stop and sputter along, never building momentum and inertia toward the chosen goal.

Stopping and Starting and ¾ Baked Thinking

People often undermine their own momentum by stopping and starting work even when things are going well. They stop to check their email or social media constantly, they quit early from work merely because a day was productive, and so on. They get up and socialize with peers or simply switch to working on something else even though they're making great progress. But each time you start and stop, it takes time to get back to where you left off cognitively. Sometimes that is easy, but other times it dulls your momentum significantly. Momentum really is the key to getting things done, and that's why it's critical to minimize distractions when you're working on something. Close your door so people can't interrupt, wear a noise-canceling headset to drown out ambient noise, turn off notifications on your phone and other devices, and just be present in the work you're doing. Momentum is a flow of energy to be cherished.

When you feel like you have momentum, try to keep it going. It might make sense to cancel other meetings or activities so you can keep your focus on driving forward. The goal is to work hard when momentum is on your side; like the current pushing the canoes, this is the best time to double down, minimize distractions, and crank. Put in extra time at work if you can, and just let the flow continue to flow. And if your work requires others, then get them to rally around and help as well. People make the mistake of stopping prematurely, thinking, *Well, it's been going great, so I can stop now*. That's the wrong approach! You'll know when it's time to stop when the work gets hard again, when the momentum shifts and things no longer come easy. That's the time to break and wait in the canoe.

When momentum stalls—and it will—don't fight it. Take a break, go for a walk, exercise, and be out in nature. Use this time to do chores or things that don't require you to think much. Do something fun! All those activities are known to shorten time when work and creativity are in ebb. The last thing you should do, unless your deadline is imminent, is force things to the point where your task becomes unbearable. Doing so will likely result in a significant drop in the quality of your work and can lead to burnout if you do it too often.

And here's another key part of the ¾ baked secret: **when your work is becoming hard, that's the time when you should share it with others.** Get feedback! Show what you've done so far and ask for help. Sometimes merely talking about your work is enough to relight the fire, or something your peer, mentor, or collaborator shares might unlock a new perspective that allows you to begin anew.

¾ baked moments are moments when you get your ideas out in the world to let the universe help perfect them. They often coincide with the point when momentum really shifts, as if the universe is telling you to stop and share!

Another way to think about this use of momentum is to consider how lactic acid builds up in your body when you exercise vigorously. If you run hard, at first you feel good and go fast; but soon, unless you pace yourself, your arms and legs get heavier and heavier and the effort finally compels you to stop. It takes time for your body to clear the lactic acid out of your bloodstream, and it does so by resting, not by continuing to work.

Momentum Surfing

The art of feeling when you have momentum in your work and maximizing what you get done during those times, then switching off to do other things when you lose momentum, is what I call *momentum surfing* (see Figure 6.1). The beautiful thing about momentum surfing is that just by working smarter, not harder, you can get a great deal more done. And, like the tennis player, if you have momentum, double down on it. Over time, with practice, the crests of the waves grow in frequency and duration and the ebb tides or troughs diminish.

Notice patterns when you can! What seemed to give you momentum the last few times? Did working in a certain place or setting help? Did you get distracted or pulled in too many directions? To surf as long as possible, use observation to adapt and change your strategy as

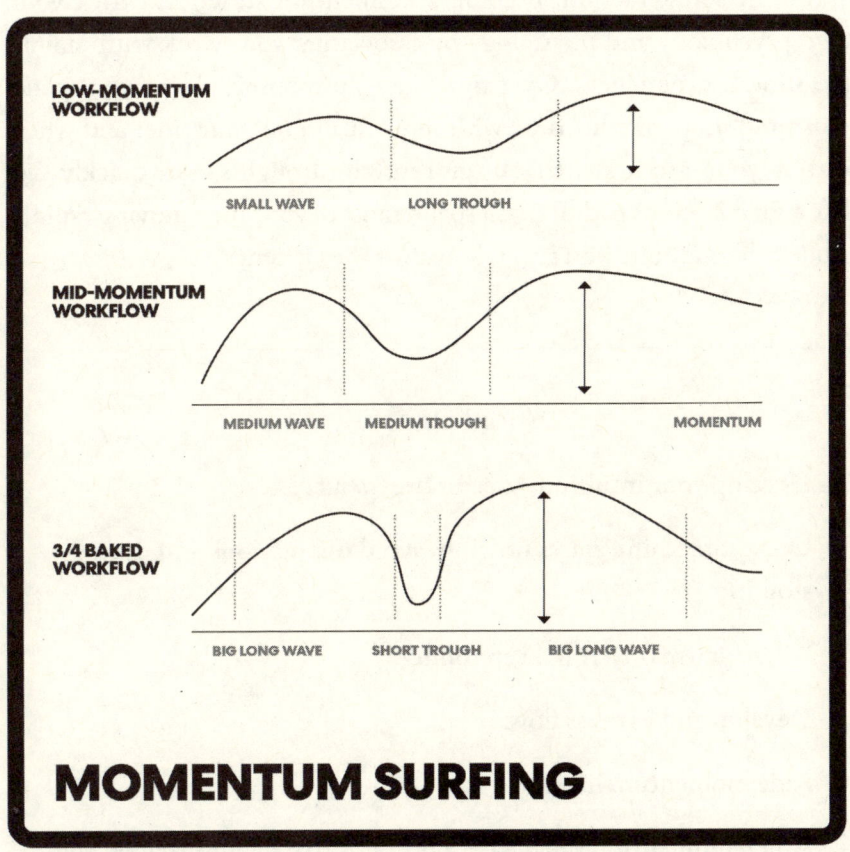

FIGURE 6.1: Momentum ebbs and flows naturally, but through practice you can increase the time when productivity is high (big waves) and decrease the time when productivity is low (troughs), getting considerably more work done.

needed. Over the years, I've cultivated this practice and noticed significant improvements in productivity while also enjoying my work more. People always wonder how I get so much done, and this is a key part of why I do. I see some of my colleagues struggle with this and get in their own way far too often. If every time you work on something it becomes an uphill climb, you're not going to enjoy it for long. And it builds negative muscle memory until people start believing things about themselves that are not true, such as, *I'm not a good writer; it's always hard for me*, or *I have a hard time getting things done; I'm no good with finishing*. These self-misconceptions become self-fulfilling prophecies.

So, in counteraction, become a momentum surfer and trick your own psychology and physiology by associating your work with mainly pleasurable experiences. Over time, like a pro tennis player, you spend more and more of your time with momentum on your side; and when it's not, you learn to switch it up and end the droughts more quickly. Or, like a First Nations paddler, you spend most of your time moving rapidly while others around you struggle against the current.

¾ BAKED SECRET

Develop your intuition; success begets success.

Once something starts flowing, avoid distractions and don't stop it.

When you're on a roll, keep rolling.

Develop and harness flow.

Ride momentum like the wind.

When momentum stalls, take a break or share your progress and watch it start anew!

Momentum Surfing and Writing

I'll take a minute to give you a sense of how I use momentum surfing in my writing. A mistake a lot of writers make, I believe, is to constantly edit while they write in the hopes of getting each sentence, each paragraph, or each chapter "perfect" before they move on to the next one. The problem with that approach is that they end up shutting down the creative flow of their work by frequently switching mental modes from writing to editing and back again. They get bogged down seeking that elusive perfect combination of words, which is why it takes some people forever to write even short passages. There are many aspiring writers who can't seem to get past a few chapters of the book they so desperately want to write, because they get stuck and ultimately too frustrated to continue. Constantly killing their creative momentum this way can lead to writer's block.

I once worked with a talented writer who had a love-hate relationship with his craft—he both loved it dearly and tortured himself with it in his constant pursuit of perfection. I had the opportunity to read first, second, and third drafts of many things he had written, and each successive draft was good but not necessarily better than the first one—just different. Sometimes it was even worse. He would constantly rewrite, thinking that he could keep improving his work, and the result was that it—and he—truly suffered. He was always throwing away his work without learning from it and starting over. His first version was in fact totally fine; he just needed someone else to help edit it rather than to keep reworking it himself. This is not to say that you don't sometimes need multiple drafts of things—I would argue that you likely *do* need several drafts to get something good—but, as we've discussed, letting go and having others edit your work is much healthier. Even when editing yourself, **when you edit is critical.** You edit in the troughs, never in the waves.

When I write, I deliberately keep the editor in me at bay. I just write—no matter how bad, scattered, or unorganized it is—and keep going until I get tired or stuck. Only then do I go back and tidy it up, fix sentences, and do basic editing—not trying to make it perfect, just good enough that others can read it and get what I'm trying to convey. Usually I get inspired to write more, so as soon as it's roughly conveying what I want it to (¾ baked, remember), I move on to the next set of ideas and ride the momentum again. The more you get down on the page, the easier it is to edit and fix it later!

Writing should be like surfing a long wave where you don't stop to edit—editing is what you do when you fall off your board.

CHAPTER 7

Slaves to Process

I am a man of fixed and unbending principles,
the first of which is to be flexible at all times.

— EVERETT DIRKSEN

CONTINUOUSLY REINVENTING THE WHEEL is inefficient. To make progress, we develop systems, procedures, and rules of thumb on which we can rely again and again. Yet these systems can both enable or hinder accomplishments and efficiency. It's difficult to get much done without some type of system, but paradoxically, the very machinery that helps move things forward often can cripple true progress, revolutionary developments, and profound change.

I've seen a lot of good ideas get bogged down in bureaucratic processes, and a lot of talented people get sidetracked within the systems they set up to make decisions. What starts out as efficiency improvements begins to take on a life of its own to the point where further progress is stymied. This sequence is typical of any great movement, business, or organization. In the start-up stages, things are chaotic and fast moving, and participants remain flexible because they have no choice. Then structures begin to fall into place that support the growth of the organization or cause and help to weed out inefficiencies. In many cases, these structures transform as they become institutionalized. Ultimately, processes, procedures, rules, and systems begin to dominate the mission, and catastrophic imbalance sets in. The result: an inevitable decline. Conversely, enduring movements and entities recognize that systems need to change as new realities emerge.

Nature provides us with wonderful examples of how not to get stuck in habitual patterns of behavior, as change is necessary for survival. As a tree grows, it adjusts constantly to respond to external forces. Each year brings a slightly different level of growth to different parts of the tree as rainfall and climate conditions vary annually. Boughs reach in new directions depending on the amount of available light and the proximity of nearby trees, which are also adjusting on a constant basis. In essence, the tree redefines its process at every moment because of ever-changing input. If a tree grew the same way every year, it would be markedly less successful.

If only human-made systems were so elegant.

As the saying goes, when you only have a hammer, everything looks like a nail. When we aim for big change, process is enormously important. Without some sort of operating rules, nothing organized and effective will happen and change will seldom occur. But when there's a disproportionate amount of focus on process, it's easier for us to lose track of our goals.

¾ BAKED SECRET

Don't spend too much time pondering how something should be accomplished—that can be just as destructive as spending too little.

Spend most of your energy on the actual effort rather than on the approach to the effort. The systems we use are not the result.

Plan quickly and be prepared to change your plans. Be nimble.

Old Dogs, Old Tricks, Old Results

We know that change is really the only constant. That truism is vividly evident every year with significant changes to technology, societal trends and patterns, and climate and geopolitics. Our world is constantly on the move. Yet surprisingly, year after year, people and industry attempt to solve challenges as if it were yesterday rather than today. Even when groups of people have the best intentions, self-limiting factors emerge in how they attempt to mobilize, make changes, or sway decisions. Old habits die hard, after all. Unfortunately for all of us, the very patterns of behavior that we have difficulty shaking are what cause most of the problems and create barriers to getting things done.

The bottom line here is that when we want a different result, we must approach the problem differently than we have in the past. Obvious, perhaps, but difficult to apply to real-world challenges. Architect William McDonough has said, "Design is the first signal of human intention." I would add that it is the systems we put in place that allow our intentions to succeed or fail. Reflection, I believe, is the signal for effective change. To be successful, we must check all of our assumptions at the door and reevaluate the way we do things. How do we make decisions as individuals? How does our group do so? What rules are already in place? Do those rules work, given the goals at hand? Is the effort effective? What new information should we use to inform our thinking and our systems?

Consider some examples from the field:

- I've seen architects who are wholeheartedly interested in transforming the environmental impacts of their building designs, yet do so without stopping to change their approach to design. They assume somehow that their *intention* is enough; that merely "willing" a green project to happen or simply tacking on green features at the end of the design process will yield the right results. Not surprisingly, the results are always less than stellar, and these designers can't understand why. Even worse, they begin to believe that their goals were never achievable. If you want a different outcome, changing how you do something is mandatory.

- I've seen design professionals whose clients push them toward better design, but they resist because the approach requires a new way of thinking, new materials, and new systems. Their disbelief in the potential success of any new reality leads them to hedge their bets, and they end up with an even more conservative, less green product than they would have had if they simply had tried.

- I've seen well-meaning not-for-profit groups get together, driven by a sense of great urgency about an issue, only to spend months discussing and arguing about *how* they should make decisions, what they believe in, and how they should communicate their beliefs. In the end, they have done very little and acted with very little urgency. Spend most of your time on actual work, and only as much time on process as absolutely necessary, knowing it will change as conditions change. This realization should make process itself less sacred.

- I've seen socially progressive companies that are driven more by a desire to build consensus and "keep everyone happy" than by the desire to accomplish the goals at hand and do excellent work. Such "designs by committee" usually result in mediocre solutions, even when highly talented people are involved. Working independently, these same participants could have produced more valuable results in half the time.

¾ BAKED SECRET

If a given approach is not working, change it.

If it is only working somewhat, tweak it.

If it works as intended, stick with it.

Repeat as often as needed.

Taking Process with a Grain of Salt

Process is no more than a tool within the ¾ baked philosophy. When it doesn't help us get the job done, we should set it aside and replace it with a more effective implement. For some reason, though, we struggle with changing protocols that feel fundamental to the way we do things. Pride, fear, and laziness all stand in the way, even when we know something must change. Many companies and institutions pride themselves on having a "system" that codifies how they do what they do. This might be fine for manufacturing (until better technologies arise) but can become dogma more than effective ethos.

When we get past the point of simply needing change for its own sake and we are ready to create the actual product or change we seek, here are some ways to stir the process pot:

DON'T TAKE ANY PROCESS TOO SERIOUSLY. Process has no intrinsic value except for the result to which it leads. There's usually more than one way to do things. The amount of time you spend figuring out a process is irrelevant if that process is no longer working. If you find yourself justifying a system simply because it took a great deal of time to create and you feel you must honor the work invested in designing it, that's a red flag. If the system isn't working, fix it.

LET GO OF EGO. Group dynamics sometimes dictate that the stronger, louder voices are the only ones heard, and those occupying the ladder's lower rungs are less worthy of attention. But flawed systems are often legacies of prior leaders and old thinking. So be sure to listen to the input of all players, remembering that the best idea, whatever its origin, benefits the entire group and furthers the cause. The point is not that everyone has an equal vote, but that everyone's ideas receive equal consideration. The best idea wins.

DON'T ASSOCIATE YOURSELF WITH THE PROCESS. Sometimes people fall in love with the processes they use to the extent that they even identify personally with them. "This is just how I do it" or "Our group has always done it this way" can be dangerous excuses, particularly when they lead to poor results. The process should lead to the goal, not limit its success. Successful individuals disassociate themselves from their processes and procedures and remain nimble. They can view the process objectively as a means to an end. Even following the advice of this book should be done with nuance and careful assessment!

KEEP THE LID TO THE TOOL KIT OPEN. If you need a hammer and all you have is a screwdriver, you don't keep trying to screw in the nail. If a process worked perfectly the last time, by all means, use it again. But if it worked in a less-than-ideal fashion, then abandon it and create a new way that takes you closer to your desired outcome. Look at how others—even or especially your competitors—do things. For profound change to occur, we must realize that there are exceptions to all systems, protocols, and rules and, with creativity, many ways to achieve a goal. Doing something out of comfort or familiarity is fine only to the extent that it doesn't hold you back from something greater.

The Pros and Cons of Dynamic Governance: A Process Case Study

In some social justice and environmental organizations, there's a trend toward a process known as *dynamic governance*, which is an effort to make group decisions with many stakeholders fair and balanced. As a tool, it can be very useful to move a contentious issue to resolution, especially to unite disparate groups and build consensus.

Here's how it works: Dynamic governance allows discussion and proposals to proceed until the group makes a decision to which nobody has a paramount objection. If anyone—even a single individual in a large group—objects, then the group continues the dialogue until it achieves a resolution that is palatable to everyone. The underlying philosophy is inclusiveness and a desire to bring everyone to a point of consensus and decision. It is a politically correct way to create solutions, and in certain instances can be highly effective. It is usually presented with the best intentions, and it is unquestionably set up to treat everyone fairly.

The problem is that too many groups use it as their sole means of making decisions, often with a negative long-term impact.

Constantly sticking to a process where everyone has an equal voice, and a single individual can hold up group decisions, places too much importance on not offending. The process begins to highjack the result. The hard truth is that not everyone's opinion is of equal value in all situations. Consensus can produce mediocre results when more powerful options are available. Even more problematic is when the vested interests of a few individuals hold back progress. Sometimes, in our efforts to treat all players fairly, we dishonor the levels of contributions people make. In this way, dynamic governance tends to prevent truly innovative ideas from taking shape, since they often come with risk and generate objections within group settings. The truth is that dynamic governance, like other decision-making systems (Robert's Rules of Order for nonprofits and local governments, for example), works in many settings—but not every setting. As leaders, we must recognize that systems and processes must cater to the challenge at hand and be adjusted to meet the challenge. A single organization might use multiple decision-making protocols over the course of one meeting if necessary and beneficial, as long as the process itself does not begin to take too long. Deciding how you are going to decide, for example, should be done quickly. I've seen some groups spend hours trying to decide how they'll make a decision! It's useful to visualize the end goal first, then work backward from that ideal scenario in order to design the most suitable process (this process, known as *backcasting*, is described in detail in Chapter 8). Create a system, test it, and recreate it if necessary.

Wu Wei and Watery Perfection

Nothing is softer or more flexible than water,
yet nothing can resist it.

—LAO TZU

When people get stuck in a rut or refuse to change their approach to problem solving, I often think of the Taoist concept of *Wu Wei*. Wu Wei has multiple interpretations, most of which deal with the notion of "effortless action," but it is universally associated with flexibility and openness to change. As such, it is the perfect philosophy to adopt when thinking about process.

Water, with its yielding nature, is the traditional symbol of Wu Wei (see Figure 7.1). Paradoxically, water is soft enough to move, yet hard enough to overpower even the most substantial stones and metals. It is formless, never forcing its own shape upon other substances and always traveling along the most efficient path. As conditions change, it even adjusts its structure from liquid to gas or solid. Always in balance, water forever finds its own level state.

WU WEI

FIGURE 7.1: Wu Wei means "inaction" or "effortless action" in Mandarin Chinese.

What a beautiful way to look at process. When we attempt to fit problems into certain systematic shapes that do not accommodate them, we may as well try to keep water from rolling off a stone. Once we learn to reshape our processes to suit the problems we face, they will prove to be watertight.

David Trubridge and the Pitfalls of Perfectionism

A super-talented individual I collaborate with from time to time is the New Zealand artist, lighting designer, and businessman David Trubridge. David is known around the world for creating a series of beautiful nature-inspired lights that take three-dimensional shape from simple, repeating two-dimensional elements. I've included his work in my home and office and with other clients. David, like me, is a true believer in the magic of imperfection and practices his own version of a ¾ baked philosophy where he doesn't let process take over. David tells a wonderful story of how he came to learn the approach as a woodworker in the 1970s and found the balance between pursuing perfection and getting paid enough to earn a living:

> You could say I slipped sideways into being a woodworker in the early 70s. I'd made a lifestyle choice living in the country, without any clear ideas about how to support that lifestyle. After renovating an old stone building in the north of England, I realized that the woodwork tools I had acquired to make doors and windows could also be put to use making furniture. So I taught myself the craft—and later design—of woodworking. I was inspired by the craft revival artisans of that era, in particular James Krenov, whose books channeled the idealism of the times into the act of turning a tree into a cherished object. I was initially one of many such acolytes, both in Britain and America (and Australia/New Zealand, I later discovered).
>
> The core of Krenov's message was a reverence for wood, with meticulous care and attention to detail. In many of his followers, these traits sadly often became obsessions. The focus became too much on the process and the wood itself. Unfortunately, this often blinded them

to the practical realities of earning a living from their craft. Some, unable to rationalize their idealism and refused to compromise, ended up teaching or as lab technicians in tertiary education. Quite soon I saw the "rabbit hole" that Krenovian "wood reverence" (as I called it) was taking us down, and I escaped.

I came to see Krenov as a red herring, diverting our attention from other aspects of furniture making, like concept/design, and in particular earning a decent living. His philosophy created the response in many makers that it doesn't matter how long it takes as long as you get it right. The problem with this preciousness, or even fanaticism, is that you now have a ridiculous amount of hours invested in an object. You can't charge all those hours at a respectable rate, so you either massively cut your rate and almost give it away; or, after being greatly admired in an exhibition with an enormous price tag, it gets taken back to your home and you have earned nothing.

David created his own "reductio ad absurdum" argument:

Consider a $2,000 egg cup. Isn't that a bit expensive for an egg cup? Well, not necessarily to the maker who spent dozens of hours turning it on a lathe from a large tree trunk. What I came to see is that every object within the craft and design world (not the art world!) has an intrinsic value, which is a combination of its utility value plus any added value you can give it, such as your reputation, your level of craft, or the materials used.

David has gone on to create a very successful career out of designing and making furniture and, of course, lighting. He understood that in business there's a price point you can charge for something within a going market rate, as shown in Figure 7.2. The longer you work at something, the less money you make, or you possibly even lose money—which is not a good business strategy! Stop too soon (half baked), and the work is shoddy and no one will want it either. There is truly a sweet spot, or break-even point. As David describes, "I learnt early when to stop and put aside the 600-grit sandpaper, when a joint fit was visibly acceptable.

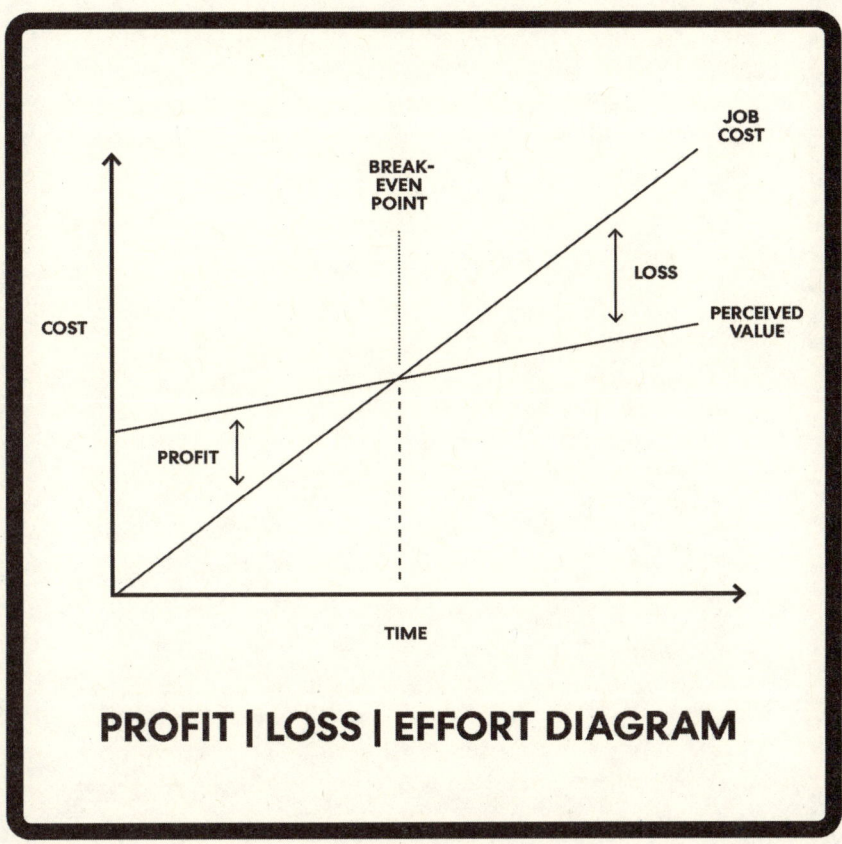

PROFIT | LOSS | EFFORT DIAGRAM

FIGURE 7.2: Profit and loss versus effort. (Used with permission from David Trubridge.)

Only a perfectionist woodworker might notice, but the client will be happy and so will my family!"

David's concept of time and value, and how profitability and loss relate, applies to nearly every business.

CHAPTER 8

Backcasting for Success

*If plan A doesn't work, the alphabet has 25
more letters—204 if you're in Japan.*

— CLAIRE COOK

AS YOU BEGIN TO PRACTICE THE MAGIC of imperfection secrets, you may find that you're completing work faster and with better results. Soon, you'll want to start planning more work this way and use the approach for strategic and long-range planning for yourself and groups you're involved with. As you do so, there are further techniques that you can layer in to help amplify your results.

Endgame Thinking

It's critically important to understand the real objective or desired result of any goal or objective you have. Take writing a report, for example. On a surface level, completing the report is the goal, but that's a shallow indicator of true success. Mere completion is not a result, except in the realm of childhood participation ribbons. Behind every deliverable should be key objectives. What is your desired impact for the work? What is it supposed to change? How is it intended to affect would-be readers? What is the larger purpose that the work is in service to? Not every report must have ambitious goals, but if there isn't some larger purpose, then why do it?

Being very clear on the "endgame" before the start of any project is fundamental to the ¾ baked philosophy, because it ensures that you keep your eye on the ball. How can you know if you've reached the ¾ mark when you don't even know what fully baked would look like?

Tied to the importance of always having a deadline should be having clarity on the endgame for anything you do. That way, as you work, you can attune your efforts to the real purpose of the work, and you won't get pulled in contradictory directions. This helps ensure that your preciously created efforts are serving the goal or mission intended and not at cross purposes to it. Knowing the endgame allows you to continue to "tack" back toward it when you're in the midst of the work.

It's surprising how little time people often spend at the outset to ask, "What is the true goal for this work?" or "How will doing this matter, and to whom?" A fuzzy sense of the desired result often leads to significant misplaced effort, or worse, a completed product that doesn't solve what it was intended to address. Being as clear as possible on what the endgame is allows us to edit out things that are extraneous and to streamline our efforts to focus on what is essential.

The Power of Alignment

When multiple people work on a project together, it's inevitable that they'll have different views of what the assignment is and how best to do it. Worse still, they often have a very different sense of what success looks like and the intended goals and outcomes of the project. Even small differences can quickly compound so that people are working at cross purposes to each other, resulting in inefficiencies, team dynamic issues, and *mission drift*, where the team loses sight of the project's original focus.

You can think of mission drift this way: when you stand on shore and watch two boats leave the harbor, it might seem like they're headed in the exact same direction, but even a slight degree of difference between them means that after a short time they'll end up very far apart (see Figure 8.1).

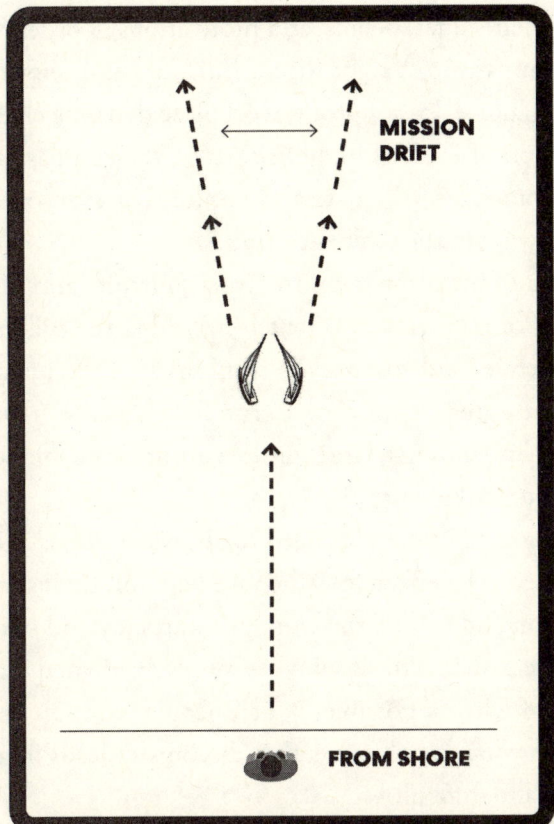

FIGURE 8.1: Viewed from shore, the two boats are headed in the same direction, but in reality, unless they keep tacking they'll soon be far apart—a useful metaphor for mission drift.

One or both boats must constantly adjust, or tack, to maintain their relative position to each other, both headed in the same direction. That is why all parties need to be in close agreement as to what the endgame or destination is for any given enterprise, as that's the gauge for how to tack or adjust within groups, a process known as *alignment*.

Kevin Hydes, a close business associate of mine and the CEO of a successful international engineering practice for many years, would often refer to *alignment* as one of the most important words in business. He would say how it's not enough to have talented people; they have to be aligned in their values, beliefs, and motivations in order for the projects and the company itself to be successful. Not being aligned is a recipe for problems—failure, loss of profit, workplace dynamic challenges, and more. It's the job of leadership, he felt, to be the compass and to keep looking for moments to evaluate and ensure that everyone is aligned, and indeed, rowing in the same direction.

The mantra of his company was "Trust, nurture, and inspire." This was a great set of core values to which he added the pillars "Imagine, perform, accelerate, and sustain." In combination, the mantra and the pillars provided a great framework to run his company. It was all about keeping alignment among a large, diverse group of people separated by geography but united in purpose.

Even if it's a team of one, we need to always be aligned to our inner purpose in order to be effective. When we work on things in alignment with our passion and values, the work generates joy and sparks creativity. Joining forces with others who are similarly aligned is a powerful amplification of what is possible. When people work on things out of alignment with what they believe, that disconnect leads to anxiety, loss of motivation, and difficulty.

So, endgame thinking is not a "one and done" approach to planning—it's essential at the outset, yes, but then we must also constantly monitor it over time to ensure that we're continually adjusting our efforts to new realities and pivoting to stay true to the course.

Backcasting versus Forecasting

Forecasts usually tell us more about the forecaster than of the future.

—WARREN BUFFETT

At the outset of every project, take time to think through what the point of it is. If the project ultimately doesn't serve a purpose, perhaps it shouldn't be started. Doing unnecessary work is folly. If the project won't really address what's needed, perhaps it needs to be redefined at a minimum.

If, however, you're clear on the endgame and have alignment and buy-in from your partners, then it's time to plan and design a strategy for completion that takes you efficiently and effectively toward the envisioned outcome. We have already been unpacking various key strategies around how to do this, but for the planning process itself there is a useful strategy called *backcasting* (see Figure 8.2).

Most people have heard of forecasting, which, simply put, is planning by thinking ahead to the next steps needed, based on where you are now. It can be effective at times, but ultimately it's limited in its value.

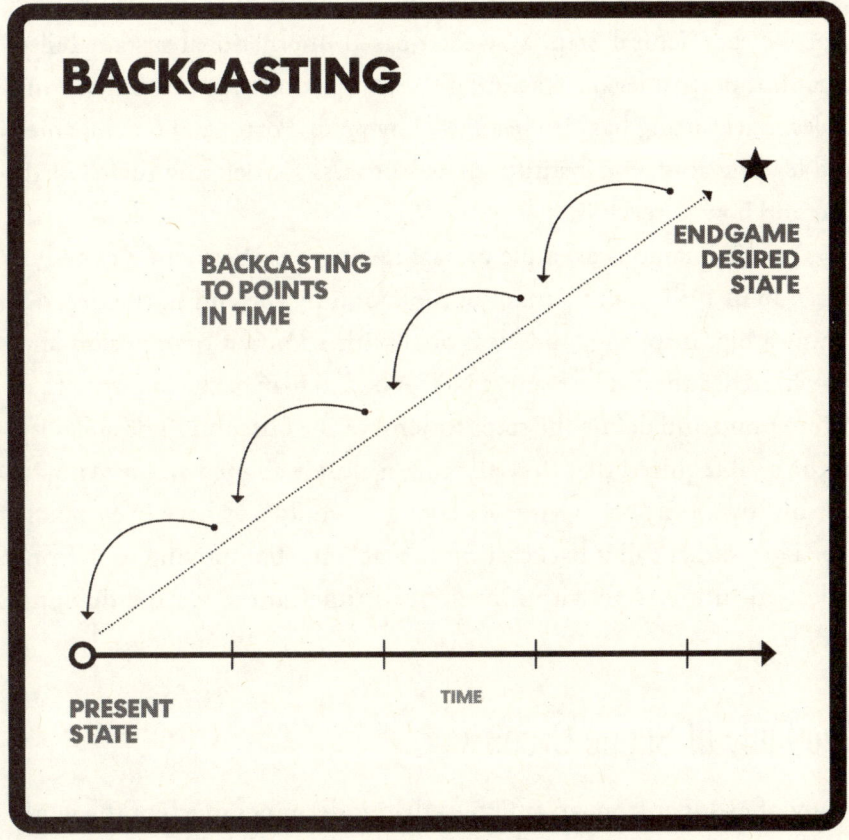

FIGURE 8.2: The backcasting process pioneered by the Natural Step involves always planning with the desired end goal in mind and working backward from that.

Backcasting is a powerful planning philosophy whereby you start with your desired endgame vision, pair it with a deadline (the time you have to complete it), and then work *backward* to the present in order to understand what has to happen to achieve the ultimate goal within the time available.

Backcasting quickly reveals when an assignment is unrealistic and unachievable, which is better to understand at the outset of a project than weeks into the work. It also gives you a great sense of focus from the beginning, as you can identify realistic interim steps and tie them to realistic interim deadlines, allowing you to constantly tack and stay aligned to the mission at hand.

First coined by John B. Robinson in 1982, backcasting has been used by many organizations successfully, including where I learned of the process: the Natural Step, a Sweden-based international sustainability organization that used backcasting to create its core sustainability principles. Backcasting has also been used by many Fortune 500 companies and leading academic institutions as a process for defining their North Star and how to reach it.

The most famous example of backcasting was President Kennedy's decision in 1961 to put a man on the moon by the end of the decade. It was a big, inspiring, and clear goal with a known time period and very hard deadline. The team at NASA had to plan backward from that future point and define the steps to achieve the outcome. The audacity of the goal required that they all remain closely aligned and moving in unison toward it; otherwise, achieving it would not have been possible. They didn't call it backcasting at that time, but moving back from a desired future state within prescribed timeframes was the defining feature.

The Folly of Scope Creep

Many of us suffer from an affliction that undermines much of the work done in the world today—that of the folly of expansion, or *scope creep*.

We've been both victims and perpetrators of this tendency. As people are working on an assignment, other ideas and possibilities emerge, some of which are essential additions to the work but many of which are merely tangents. Sure, they might have value, but they suddenly grow what is required, and often the deadline or the quality of work suffers from expanding the focus.

We certainly know talented people in our work life who fit the definition of serial "expanders"—people who like to grow a problem or expand the work they're doing as widely as they can. Many of them are extremely talented, but they can't seem to stay focused. I'll explain more about expanders in the appendix.

A key element of success with the ¾ baked philosophy is to stay focused on the endgame and not expand the assignment or task any more than it needs to be until you can begin to share it out with the world. An idea that makes the core mission better is not an expansion necessarily, but one that's outside of that outcome is.

By all means, take some time up front to consider if you can resolve multiple issues through the same action or if related work is relevant—doing this is good holistic thinking! But don't do it at the expense of getting the essential elements done on time to the appropriate level of completion.

When you recognize expansion work, a better approach is to write it down and put it in a "parking lot" or queue of sorts, and then consider doing it after you've met the initial deadline or, if it's simple, during a "trough" in workflow as a way of changing up your mental space. In this way, you're not ignoring good tangential ideas, but you're solving them in their proper "order of operations" sequence, as we discussed earlier. When others attempt to expand the assignment, you can acknowledge the idea, remind them of the deadline and core purpose of the work, and promise to revisit their suggestion.

Staying true to the endgame and using backcasting to ensure timely results allows us the grace to continually innovate, expand, and build—but on the back of the original success, now amplified.

¾ BAKED SECRET

Start with a clear vision for the end result desired.

Use that as a guide toward which to continuously steer your efforts.

Plan your strategy by backcasting from the endgame to the current time to ensure that efforts are attuned to timelines and thus achievable.

CHAPTER 9

Becoming a Trim Tab

So I said that the little individual can be a trim tab. Society thinks it's going right by you, that it's left you altogether. But if you're doing dynamic things mentally, the fact is that you can just put your foot out like that and the whole big ship of state is going to go. So I said, call me Trimtab.

—BUCKMINSTER FULLER

Give me a lever long enough and a fulcrum on which to place it, and I shall move the world.

—ARCHIMEDES

THIS ARCHIMEDES QUOTE IS CITED REGULARLY. Some may say it appears too frequently in business books, but it's popular because it helps to illustrate a crucial change-oriented concept: it is not enough simply to exert effort in order to make change; what matters most is *how* we go about making change. Nobody wants to work hard and achieve nothing. Identifying and utilizing the appropriate lever and fulcrum can turn effort into results. If your interest in life is to be effective at what you do and to have meaningful impact, then it's important to apply the ¾ baked philosophy in service to something greater—to be both productive and *effective* and to identify any and all opportunities to serve as a lever.

Illustrating the Point

Many years ago when I was hired as the new CEO of the Cascadia Green Building Council (now the International Living Future Institute), one of my new employees asked me what the organization was going to "be" under my direction. Instead of responding verbally, I drew the simple illustration of a piece of wood (Figure 9.1).

FIGURE 9.1: A simple piece of wood?

"What is it?" she asked, a bit perplexed.

"It's a trim tab, of course," I replied, having fun with the vagueness of my answer and the befuddlement of my new employee.

"All right, I'll bite," she said. "What's a trim tab?"

I returned to the paper and completed the drawing by adding a second piece of wood adjacent to the first and attaching both to a boat (Figure 9.2).

"You've drawn a rudder," she said, smiling. "I get it. We're going to help steer the green movement."

"Yes," I agreed. "But this metaphor means much more than that."

I went on to explain myself and my drawing. A trim tab, I told her, is a tiny rudder placed below a larger rudder on substantial ocean-going

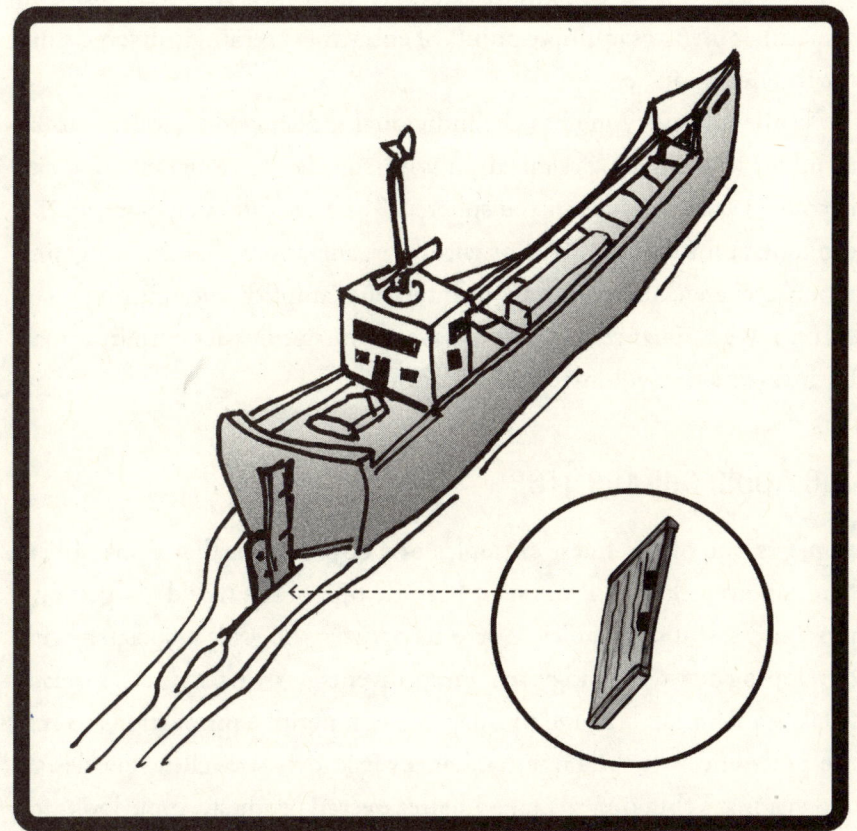

FIGURE 9.2: A trim tab on a boat is a metaphor of leverage whereby a small rudder helps a larger rudder turn a large ship.

vessels. Relative to its counterpart, the trim tab is insignificant in size. But without it, the main rudder would be useless, and the ship would be unable to turn. It is a lever acting on a lever, an intriguing example of the very principle to which Archimedes referred. But there's more to this story. In order to compel the rudder to turn the boat, the trim tab actually moves in the *opposite* direction of the rudder. To create change, it goes down a completely divergent path.

To my mind, the trim tab is the most fantastic real-world example of how individuals and organizations can accomplish change that is seemingly disproportionate to their own size and scale by steering away from the mainstream. It shows that it's possible to be a lever acting upon another lever, harnessing the efforts of much larger entities. Most importantly, it shows that the path to success is not always the straightest and sometimes involves multiple points of entry that seemingly diverge from the intended course.

While not everyone has the individual influence or resources to be a rudder (leading an organization with significant clout), anyone can become a trim tab within the sphere of influence they operate in. We can look at initiatives and ideas within organizations that are struggling to make change and seek ways to intervene, amplify, and improve their success. We can figure out how to have an outsize impact even in a small business or a tiny volunteer organization.

The Apple and the Tree

Apple is one of the finest examples of a corporation that thinks like a trim tab even though it has now become one of the world's largest and most successful companies. Apple recognizes the risks associated with developing new technology, so it rarely invents its own products. Instead, it takes a trim tab attitude by adapting competitive innovations to suit the preferences of the target audiences it knows so well, using design and visionary thinking to make a better overall product. Apple looks for the highest point of leverage, repackages products, and transforms user experiences in new and different ways.

The iPod was a powerful early example. MP3 players had been on the market for several years before Apple repurposed the technology, put a sexy new spin on the idea, tied the concept to a music purchasing site, and kicked off a global marketing phenomenon. The iPod became a trim tab for change that has overhauled the way music is bought, sold, and heard throughout the world. Apple went on to control a significant share of the global digital music player market for many years.

Apple applied the same approach when it launched the iPhone, repackaging existing technologies and ideas and revolutionizing tele-communications. In its first year on the market, the iPhone earned *Time* magazine's top invention of the year honors and now, nearly a decade and a half later, it is still the dominant technology in its space, just as the iPad and iWatch are in theirs.

A Green Trim Tab

In the green building world, the United States Green Building Council (USGBC) is the ultimate example of the trim tab concept. Established in 1996 as a unifying resource for the various factions dedicated to green building, the USGBC is now a sizeable nonprofit powerhouse that steers the entire industry. In effect, the USGBC began as a trim tab and quickly emerged as the movement's rudder.

What is particularly interesting about the USGBC story is that the organization was founded simply as a mechanism to bring together the multiple specialties within the green building community and assist them in focusing their efforts. The USGBC belonged to no one group—it was neither heavily represented nor influenced by architects, engineers, designers, contractors, or government agencies. Instead, it existed to benefit all those who participated in the green movement. Each discipline did good work but operated as a silo without a unifying set of guidelines. USGBC served as the trim tab to the building industry's rudder, uniting the specialties under one banner. But the industry was so ready for direction that the USGBC, along with the LEED standards it developed, quickly became the rudder itself. As environmentalist Paul

Hawken has publicly declared, the USGBC does more to further the green building movement and enable real change than dozens of non-governmental organizations (NGOs) combined.

Just as the USGBC led to the development of LEED standards, LEED standards opened the door to the possibility of the Living Building Challenge (LBC), the program I authored and launched back in 2006 to raise the "glass ceiling" of what is possible to achieve with building design. Now that green building practices are more widely accepted and LEED standards are more commonly met, the LBC ups the ante by asking even more of the building community. In this sense, the LBC is the trim tab on the USGBC rudder. By leveraging the recently elevated interest in green building, LBC takes it one step further and defines a greater goal—the endgame strategy for the built environment. In 1997, when LEED standards were first introduced, people felt that the platinum level was the furthest (and greenest) point to which sustainable building could be taken. LBC seeks to extend that endpoint, since the industry has proven it can meet the platinum goals on building projects all over the continent.

FIGURE 9.3: An image of one of my building designs from 2025: the new Center for Environmental Science and Sustainability for Henrico County Public Schools, aiming to be the world's first Living Building public school in Virginia. (Credit: Perkins&Will/ McLennan Design.)

By 2011, the world's first Living Buildings were certified, and since then we've seen that idea take off and spread to markets all over the world. Living Buildings generate all their own energy by renewable energy alone, without the use of any fossil fuels. They work within the water balance of their sites and local climate and capture and treat all their water on-site. They are built without the use of the toxic "red-list chemicals" often ubiquitous in other buildings and achieve a host of other environmental benchmarks that place them above all other green buildings in terms of positive environmental impact. The beautiful thing is that each built example of a Living Building often inspires others to do the same and, in so doing, becomes further leverage for positive change.

Looking Within

A soul without a high aim is like a
ship without a rudder.

— EILEEN CADDY

Acting like a trim tab requires time to think and reflect on strategic rather than merely reactive change.

Being a trim tab for change requires

- pursuing strategic collaboration with the rudders, rather than competition for competition's sake;

- complementing rather than duplicating the rudders' existing efforts;

- investing effort commensurate with the amount of desired change;

- resisting the urge to act as a rudder ourselves by tackling issues that are beyond our own resources and knowledge, thus avoiding significant wasted effort; and

- becoming comfortable with the idea of potentially countering popular sentiment, because change is not always popular.

¾ BAKED SECRET

When you're ready to act, first look to understand how your actions, skills, and contributions can do the most good.

Harness the works of others.

Look for ways to leverage change, and for opportunities for interventions that bring cascading effects.

Acting On Opportunities

Change starts when someone
sees the next step.

—WILLIAM DRAYTON

During the early years of my architectural career, I was surrounded by talented people who did important and beneficial work. I practiced within a midsize firm called BNIM Architects in Kansas City, Missouri, and we considered ourselves a firm with a mission. We devoted ourselves personally and professionally to positive societal and environmental change in every project we were involved with. Yet sometimes, despite our best efforts, projects failed. I participated in a number of significant projects that spanned several years of efforts but never ended up getting built. I often felt frustrated after working diligently for two or more years on a given job, only to have the project disappear for one reason or another (economics, politics, etc.). When these projects went away, seemingly so too did our valuable work, ideas, and designs. It always seemed to me that this kind of knowledge deserved to exist further out in the public realm, owned by more than just a single client with lots of resources.

Therefore, in 1999, I founded a consultancy called Elements, one of the first of its kind on the continent.[1] The philosophy was simple: provide sustainable consulting services to competitive design firms (and internally within BNIM) in order to broaden the industry-wide understanding of green building practices and push the knowledge outward (while making profit for our company).

At first, many thought we were crazy to assist our competitors. Surely we were giving up our "trade secrets" and relinquishing our competitive advantage! But we knew better. We understood that helping the larger goal of greening the industry was more important than protecting our professional egos. We also understood that by consulting to others, we were simultaneously making several smart business moves for our own organization:

- We were solidifying our reputation as the true "experts" in the marketplace.

- We were learning new ways to communicate the information we knew.

- We were reaching into new markets and getting exposed to significantly more project types and clients.

- We were always learning what others in our industry knew and what they didn't know, so we could stay one step ahead.

The experiment ended up being a great success, serving as an important trim tab for numerous projects all over the country while helping to grow our business internally.

From there, I looked for additional ways to leverage my knowledge and connections to enable further change. Having seen the impact Paul Hawken's books made, I founded Ecotone Publishing to ensure that information about green building was readily available to those who sought it. The lever lengthened and the fulcrum strengthened, and I published my first book, *The Philosophy of Sustainable Design*, which has been used in over one hundred universities and colleges across the continent and is available for purchase globally. Through Ecotone, I published the works of other experts and extended the reach and quality of the green building message. Ecotone today is still the only dedicated "green building publisher" and, now owned by the International Living Future Institute, produces several important new titles each year.

My decision to join and lead a not-for-profit was rooted in my belief that I need to do all I can to continue the momentum of these message-spreading exercises. As the reality of climate change and other globally significant environmental challenges has become more apparent, organizations such as the International Living Future Institute present the opportunity to help hundreds of firms from all backgrounds in their green efforts. But the leaders of these organizations must be willing to let go of a certain amount of ego and personal gratification and allow the success of others to take the spotlight. Just as an architect creates tangible works that incorporate and display their design talents, an educator enables others to grow and shine and must be satisfied with that background role. Much like a trim tab.

¾ BAKED SECRET

Remember, regardless of where you are in your career, there are always opportunities to make change.

Look for them.

And try to find places to intervene where you can leverage your skills and knowledge.

Do not hesitate—begin.

Steering Yourself toward Change

The entrepreneur always searches for change,
responds to it, and exploits it
as an opportunity.

— PETER F. DRUCKER

Once we have decided to act—to be moved by our passion and our beliefs—we must ask ourselves, "What next?" What kinds of actions do we take? How can we get the most strategic impact from what we do? Even leaders of corporate and government entities must ask themselves these same questions if they want to work toward meaningful change.

As you seek ways in which you can serve as a trim tab, look for the following:

- Groups or individuals doing good work but lacking in some key resource that you could provide

- Work that nobody is doing yet that would add value to a greater effort

- Work that is being done on an old paradigm that could be reinvented or recreated

- Work that needs a new "story" or medium

- Work that is already being done but for which you could help supply a new audience

- Work that is being pushed in the wrong direction that you could help steer toward a more effective solution or model

- Work that is being done well in another region or venue that you could bring closer to home

Basically, we must ask ourselves how to create new fulcrums for levers that are already in place. Creating profound change is not always about reinventing the wheel. Sometimes it's about discovering new forms of leverage.

CHAPTER 10

Nested Time on the Brain's Right Side

The best thing about the future is that it all comes one day at a time.

—ABRAHAM LINCOLN

IT'S HUMAN NATURE for us to tackle challenges by first attempting to define the problem at hand within the context of our previous experiences and existing knowledge. We can't help it; that's all we know, so that's all the information we have with which to deal with new situations. The problem with this approach, however, is that it limits us to a set of possible answers that may not be suitable for the questions we need to ask. We end up working within a construct that defines us—and imprisons us.

When we seek to make real change in our lives and in our businesses, we must begin by thinking beyond the limits of our own experiences, turning our own conventional thinking on its head.

But how do we do this?

Drawing on the Right Side

In 1979, an art teacher named Betty Edwards published a groundbreaking book called *Drawing on the Right Side of the Brain* after conducting research on the ways in which both hemispheres of the brain contribute to, as well as hinder, learning.[1] In the book, she demonstrates the powerful truth that the left side of our brain, which is devoted to logical and analytical thinking, hinders our ability to learn to draw and visualize precisely because it "thinks" it knows how to solve the problem of drawing when in fact it does not. Most people experience frustration upon attempting to draw, and very few pursue it beyond what elementary school requires. When someone says, "I can't draw," it's actually the left brain that can't draw. Edwards's techniques have shown thousands of people how to "shut off" their left brains and learn with their right brains, allowing even those with no apparent artistic talent to make dramatic leaps in creative performance in short periods of time. Techniques include drawing upside-down and obscuring elements of a picture so that the left brain doesn't try to "finish" a drawing based on what it "knows." Edwards shows what's possible when we take ourselves out of the paradigm to which we've become accustomed. Only then can we recognize the changes that need to take place. This is not to say that right brain–dominant people get it and left brain people don't—not at all. We've all seen incredibly creative people unable to function and solve simple problems because they haven't known when to change the way they think. We have two sides of our brain for a reason—and it's time that we use both.

The Time of Your Life: An Example

Time is a human-made construct that governs and restricts us. It has the power to become our greatest limiter, our biggest source of personal frustration, and the highest barrier between us and our ability to create profound change. From the time we're little, we're taught to think of time in a purely linear fashion. Like so many things in our lives, one thing happens after another, end of story, and we don't challenge it. When we look at time management from a new angle, however, we give ourselves the power to drive major change in our own lives, and this perspective is incredibly important to the ¾ baked philosophy.

It's cliché to say that time is precious; that's true of anything finite and limited. Add the increasing pace at which we insist on living and the countless tools that help us squeeze more into our days, and it's no wonder everybody feels pinched. Time is a valuable commodity, yet how many of us really look at how we spend it? Do we do all we can to get the most out of the time we have? Is there a connection between the way we spend time and the quality of our lives and our happiness? And here's a big one: Is there a significant environmental impact when we mismanage or lose track of our time? Let's look at a couple of reasons why we are so short on time.

Reason One: Temporal Parasitics

Most of us don't really understand where our time goes during any given day. To paraphrase my good friend Ron Perkins, an innovative engineer who pioneered efficiency practices in the building industry in the 1990s and 2000s, "You do not know what you do not measure, and what you do not measure you do not really understand." In our daily lives, we rarely measure how we truly spend time. A big problem for most in our culture is a phenomenon I call *temporal parasitics*.

Parasitics is an energy efficiency term used to describe equipment that draws power even when not in use. Nearly every household appliance is a parasitic load once plugged in. Prior to the introduction of flatscreen TVs, conventional television sets would draw electricity when plugged in, even while turned off, which cost the owners money and created unnecessary pollution. The primary justification for this particular parasitic was to keep the set's internal tube warm so that the picture would appear as soon as the TV was turned on rather than taking several seconds to heat up. This momentary convenience—this brief time-saving advantage—drained energy all day and all night, year-round. Was that instant gratification worth the pollution generated and money wasted to achieve it? The notion of holistic time management asks the same question.

There are a million little things that we do each and every day in order to maintain our lifestyles. Our small decisions support our big ones regarding where we live, what we do to support ourselves, and how we define success. We ignore these seemingly insignificant decisions because we consider them trivial; we think of them as unnecessary, and we don't take them into account when we make important choices. But I believe we should make them visible because, in sum, they account for the vast majority of our wasted time. They suck away time; they are temporal parasitics.

Any major life decision comes complete with a whole package of hidden temporal parasitics that are either small or large, depending on the course of action. Whatever their magnitude, they have serious implications. You need only look at the number of Americans whose financial liabilities hurl them into endless cycles of work and debt reduction to see how temporal parasitics have the capacity to ruin health, happiness, and home life. When you're in debt, you're not in complete control of your time (for more on that, I recommend reading the groundbreaking book *Your Money or Your Life: 9 Steps to Transforming Your Relationship with Money and Achieving Financial Independence* by Vicki Robin and Joe Dominguez[2]).

For many people, the decision to buy into the "American dream" has been disastrous—for their families as well as the environment—as it is often driven more by a desire for possessions and status than by genuine need. The typical dream scenario involves buying a large house in the suburbs, at least twice as big as the house the buyers grew up in (and now serving a smaller family), instead of living closer to work in a more integrated, multi-use neighborhood. This decision has led the average American to spend a significant amount of time and money each day commuting to work (and generating more emissions) and running errands made necessary by the great distances between services. Even more time is spent maintaining the oversized homes and hiring help to clean it, which of course requires more work hours to fund.

Other examples roll in:

- We accept jobs that require overtime or indirect work-related time in order to generate more income to pay for the mortgages on the big houses.

- We purchase additional vehicles to shuttle us to and from our jobs, often spending additional time looking for parking or being stuck in rush-hour traffic.

- We invest in elaborate wardrobes to support our professional positions and, because of a lack of time, we spend more time and money on dry cleaning and laundering.

- We spend more time eating out since we don't have time to cook at home.

- And the time-eating cancer grows. . . .

Like their energy counterparts, temporal parasitics usually impose an environmental burden as well. For each mile it crawls through traffic, the average gas automobile produces between 0.5 to 1.5 pounds of carbon dioxide, which also contributes to the creation of ground-level ozone, particulates, and other threats to our health. Eating "convenience" food, including prepackaged meals and menu items from fast food restaurants, is as bad for our health as it is for the environment, given the energy and resources used to package, process, and ship the food as well as the industrialized agricultural systems needed to support it.

Reason Two: Temporal Dilution

Temporal dilution refers to activities that we don't need to do, and many times don't even particularly want to do, yet we do out of habit, boredom, or stress. These activities add no value to our lives, but we seek them out nonetheless. For many people, watching television is a great example. Certainly, there can be quite valuable programming, but too many Americans and Canadians use television or streaming services like junk food, endlessly flipping channels and not digesting anything meaningful or intellectually nutritious. I call it temporal dilution because it typically refers to activities that we don't notice or account for but, bit by bit, siphon time away from more meaningful things. Email, social media, and electronic content have begun to dominate the lives of many who have replaced healthier activities with these mind-numbing activities. Many of our unproductive or unfulfilling activities occur just a little bit at a time, and therefore we don't experience their cumulative effects consciously. We're not aware in the moment how much time we spend or waste (depending on your perspective) engaging in these activities. We do know, however, that we always feel the time crunch and there never seem to be enough hours in the day to do all that we want and need to do. Temporal dilution makes it difficult for us to see the incentive to change. We justify enormous hours away: "What does it matter if I spend a couple of hours a day on social media or checking my phone messages constantly? That's not much time, and many people have habits much worse than mine."

But here's the rub: rationalizations such as these prevent us from devoting our time and living our lives the way we would like to—and being effective in the coming years ahead will require us to be much more consciously in control of our time. With temporal dilution, we don't notice things even though their cumulative effects are just as damaging to our health and well-being as if they happened all at once.

Let's begin to think on the right side of our brain and take a closer look at how we spend our time.

What if we had to lump together all the time we spend in, say, a year on each time-diluting activity and examine how our twelve-month schedule would map out? I believe that this exercise would teach us all a few things about the priorities we set and how to get on the path to becoming truly effective.

On average, every day the typical American working adult

- sleeps 7.5 hours,

- works 8 hours,

- spends 1.2 hours commuting to and from work (although this has changed for some post-pandemic),

- spends 1.1 hours (66 minutes) eating and drinking (although increasingly while commuting to and from work),

- devotes 2.6 hours to leisure and sports,

- spends 1 hour in the bathroom (doing all sorts of things),

- spends 4.3 hours looking at their phone,

- cares for others 1.2 hours,

- engages in other household activities for 1 hour, and

- spends the remaining time on miscellaneous activities.[3]

Now let's look at this another way. Say you had to perform each of these tasks in *succession* instead of in little daily or weekly increments that you don't think about, stopping only to sleep for your requisite 7.5 hours, but spending every other waking moment performing each task. What would that look like over the course of the year?

From January 1st to March 15th, you would just be sleeping, oblivious to anything else.

April would be the month spent in the bathroom doing all manner of things.

In May, you would spend all your time simply driving to and from work by yourself (since most North Americans drive alone) and during three of those days, you would spend all your waking hours completely stuck in traffic!

You would then spend the summer doing work without a break until September, when you'd simply stare at your phone, computer, or television.

Pause right there.

It is now October. Fall has arrived, and you still haven't spent any quality time with your kids, with your spouse, or for yourself. And sadly, when you do carve out those times, you end up with less than a month for each (see Figure 10.1). What's wrong with that picture?

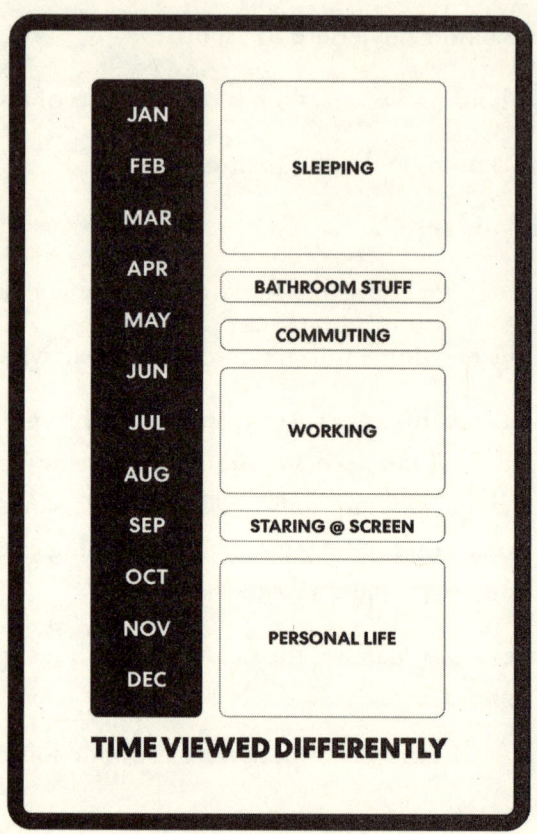

FIGURE 10.1: How your year would look if you had to do certain activities continuously rather than spread out.

How do you spend your time? If these were your patterns, would you make profound changes on your own behalf or for your kids? If you learned that you spent a significant portion of your time in ways that also used considerable energy and increased your ecological footprint, would you find it easier to change? When you look at your time-use patterns, ask yourself how your job choice affects your time. How does where you live affect the hours you spend doing things you don't want to do (such as commute)? Are there activities you'd like to be able to spend more time doing? The key is to be aware of things that take time and have a ripple effect, drawing on your physical and emotional reserves and making you less effective in other areas.

The sad reality is that we don't notice life passing us by when it does so in little increments. As a result, we tend to make less time for the really important things because we are busy frittering away our time on the mundane—what the author Antoine de Saint-Exupéry sarcastically called "matters of consequence."

This reminds me of the life lesson made popular by the author Stephen Covey (author of *7 Habits of Highly Effective People*) in which a professor stands before his classroom with a large jar, a pile of rocks, a bag of sand, and a pitcher of water (see Figure 10.2).[4] He fills the jar to capacity with rocks, then asks the students if it is full. "Yes," they reply. "No more rocks will fit." He then adds sand, which fills the spaces between

IF YOU FILL YOUR JAR WITH GRAVEL AND SAND FIRST, YOU WON'T HAVE SPACE FOR YOUR BIG ROCKS

FIGURE 10.2: Stephen Covey popularized the metaphor of making sure to put the "big rocks" in your life first and adding the "sand" after.

the rocks. "Is it full now?" he asks. "Yes, now it is full," the students say. Finally, he adds water, which spreads easily throughout the sand. "Now this jar is full," he announces. "The moral here is clear: we must start by taking care of the big things in life—family, friends, our health, our well-being—because there will always be room for the little things, as they can take up the remaining spaces." Doing this for your life is ¾ baked thinking.

¾ BAKED SECRET

Turn thinking on its head.

When stuck in a problem, change the paradigm by turning it upside down.

Think consciously of how your opposite mind would react and cultivate both your left- and right-brain modes of problem solving.

Stretch out of your comfort zone so that you're ready to change dramatically when it's most important.

Nested Problem Solving

Every once in a while, we make decisions that seem particularly sound—decisions made in a moment of grace that help solve multiple problems at once. I like to call this type of solution *nested problem solving*, as individual answers nest within others (see Figure 10.3).

With practice, nested problem solving can become an everyday methodology in and of itself, and it has the potential to greatly increase the quality of life we all seek. Once we become aware of the interconnectedness of our daily habits, our ability to manage time and the ecological impact of our decisions, nested solutions come more easily. Please note that this is not the same thing as multitasking, which is merely doing different things

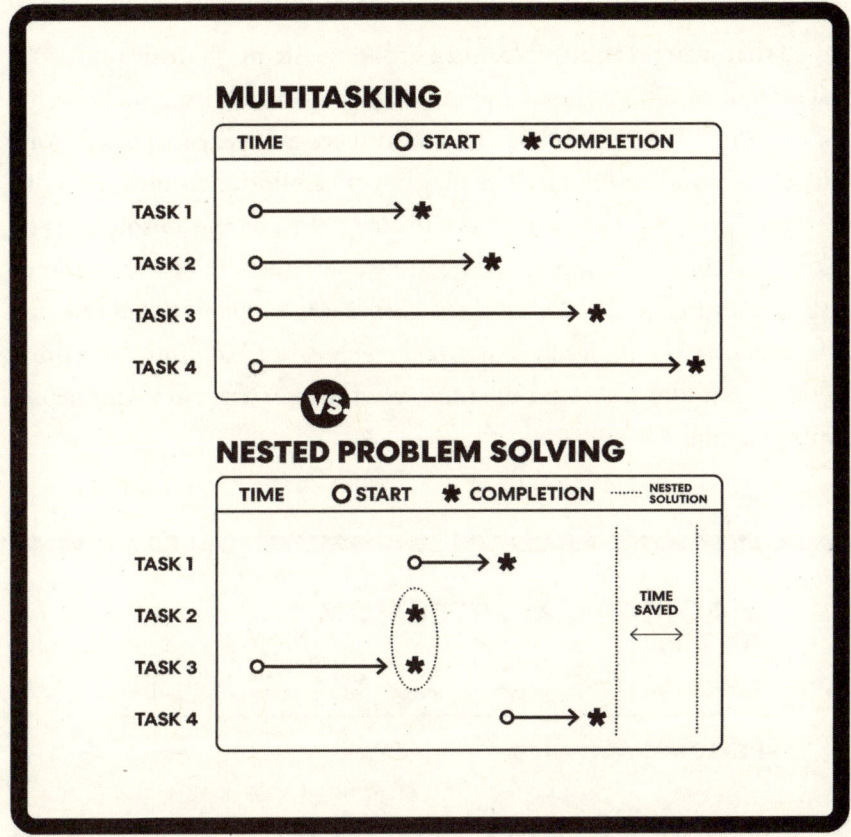

FIGURE 10.3: Comparing multitasking to nested problem solving shows the difference between doing multiple things at once—and probably poorly—and strategically looking for ways of solving one task that eliminate the need for or solve another task.

at the same time—usually none of it as well as you could if you focused on one! Nested problem solving focuses on pairing or merging activities that are synergistic and enhance the result or the enjoyment in doing them. Truly nested solutions tend to be simultaneously good for our health, our pocketbooks, and the environment. These solutions are a complete reversal from many habits that cost us a lot, have great environmental burdens, contribute to poor health, and leave us with nested problems to solve!

You can cultivate nested solutions using such simple tools as daily to-do lists (see Figure 10.4). I, for one, am a relentless list maker. As I mentioned earlier in the book, I like to take a few moments in the evening to jot down the key tasks I know I need to accomplish the following day so that, wherever possible, I can group the items on my list into logical categories. This option helps cut down on wasted time and helps me stay on track. This type of system doesn't work for everyone, but anyone who wants to streamline time management can find their most effective method of nesting solutions. You can also cultivate nested solutions by taking the time to reflect on all possible consequences of the action or task in question and asking: *Is there a better way to approach this task that is healthier, more ecologically sound, and inexpensive?* You must be willing to measure and understand the impacts of the current paradigm before simply changing it.

MAGIC OF IMPERFECTION
TO-DO LIST

TASKS	DUE DATE	JOY METER	SIGNIFICANCE METER	TIME ESTIMATE	SYNERGIES
PERSONAL ACTIVITES					
TASK 1	FRIDAY	4	4	6 hrs	✱
TASK 2	NEXT WK	3	2	4 hrs	
TASK 3	NEXT WK	2	2	16 hrs	✱
TASK 4	WEDNESDAY	1	4	1 hr	
PROJECT ONE					
TASK 1	NEXT WK	3	3	8 hrs	
TASK 2	NEXT WK	2	3	4 hrs	✱
TASK 3	NEXT WK	3	3	2 hrs	✱
PROJECT TWO					
STEP 1	AUG. 18	1	3	12 hrs	
STEP 2	AUG. 20	1	2	8 hrs	✱
STEP 3	AUG. 30	1	3	4 hrs	

FIGURE 10.4: A right brain/left brain to-do list that prioritizes tasks and identifies synergies.

Naturally, the hardest part of the process is coming up with the solution, but most people are creative enough to come up with several appropriate solutions as soon as they broaden the context. Unfortunately, many people are stuck in an all-too-common pattern, a spiraling of interconnected problems that leads to negative feedback loops. For example, the busy career person with no time to cook rarely eats at home, ironically spending almost the same time traveling to and from restaurants, often choosing unhealthy and environmentally disastrous fast food or packaged foods, and spending at least twice the amount of money for nutritionally diminished fare. The person stuck in this pattern ends up needing to work more to pay for their habit of eating out, and the stressful, wasteful cycle continues.

¾ BAKED SECRET

Be brave and look for the ideal solution in every endeavor.

Look for solutions to life's challenges that are healthy, environmentally sound, and economically wise.

Slow down, think about simplicity, and make each decision count.

Practice mindfulness.

We need to look for synergistic activities or synergistic ways of accomplishing our goals. The Buddhist Thich Nhat Hanh talks about using the mundane to practice the profound, not by multitasking but by focusing on the task at hand. As he says, "When washing the dishes one should only be washing the dishes."[5] Mindfulness is necessary to recognize nested solutions.

Making Risotto

*To my mind, the idea that doing the dishes is
unpleasant can occur only when you are not doing
them. Once you are standing in front of the sink
with your sleeves rolled up and your hands in
warm water, it really is not so bad. I enjoy taking
my time with each dish, being fully aware of the
dish, the water, and each movement of my hands. I
know that if I hurry in order to go and have a cup
of tea, the time will be unpleasant and not worth
living. That would be a pity, for each minute, each
second of life is a miracle.*

— THICH NHAT HANH

Whenever I can, I take the time to cook an incredibly elaborate meal at home. I especially enjoy the act of chopping and preparing the ingredients, relishing the fresh raw scent of vegetables, onions, and garlic on my hands. Although we have a garlic press, I don't use it when preparing one of these feasts. I prefer to work by hand with an extra-sharp knife, cutting and slicing and setting each ingredient aside until I have a beautiful tray ready for cooking—the mise en place. For me, these culinary projects are all about delving fully and completely into the task of preparing food for my family and enjoying the process of turning raw ingredients into melded and enriched tastes through cooking. I simply lose myself in it, and it makes for a powerful metaphor for the idea of nested problem solving. While cooking "slow food," I am

- pursuing a treasured leisure activity;

- allowing myself time for reflection and stress relief;

- sharing this work (and the fruits of the labor) with loved ones;

- contributing to my health by using quality organic ingredients; and

- reducing my environmental footprint, since hand-prepared, seasonal, and locally sourced meals have less of an environmental impact than "quick and simple" packaged dishes with ingredients from all corners of the planet.

One of my best friends, who has seen me in my soiled apron and who shares my appreciation for cooking, describes the process of taking the time to do things right as "making risotto," as a proper risotto is notoriously time-consuming to make but can be quite delicious. I now use the phrase as a metaphor describing the action of losing yourself in any function that promotes quality of life and serves as a nested solution for health, environmental benefit, and human interaction. For me, "making risotto" can be as simple as taking an extra-long walk with my dog. Sometimes it is sitting down with a cup of tea and reading a good book for a solid hour instead of watching TV. Making risotto is a directive to slow down, allow time to think, and become proactive rather than reactive to our daily routines. Amazing things happen when we turn down our energy levels and do things more slowly and deliberately—ironic for a book about getting things done. Sometimes the key is taking a break from work long enough to get centered.

¾ BAKED SECRET

Take time to make risotto in all aspects of life. Add flair and beauty to the tasks you face, and revel in your ability to put your personal stamp on your creations.

Have fun with the little jobs you do, which make you better able to appreciate the more significant accomplishments that come along.

Enjoy the present—that's all we have.

Needless to say, making risotto is a metaphor for good living. In the proverbial rat race, there is little time for anything but consumption and so-called progress without time for reflection and strategic planning. We are reactive rather than proactive, which means we rarely have the time to craft elegant and intelligent solutions.

CHAPTER 11

The Magic of the ¾ Baked Team

If I have seen further, it is by standing on the shoulders of giants.

—ISAAC NEWTON

WHILE THIS IS NOT A BOOK about managing people and teams, it's important to spend some time on the subject since, per the ¾ baked secret, very little that is truly excellent gets done in isolation; it takes the universe (others) to fully bake most things. Great work requires great teams. And I would put forward that there is also a "sweet spot" for how teams work, and for the interplay and dynamics of the people within the team, that is needed to produce great results. There is, in fact, an ideal "¾ baked team"—one whose members are collaborating tightly, working together synergistically, and calibrating efforts and outcomes efficiently.

Key Principles for Team Success

A lot has already been written on how to create great teams—and going into detail on this would likely merit another book—so I'll just mention a few key principles that are fundamental to a ¾ baked team success:

MAINTAIN A "NO ASSHOLES" POLICY. Whether talented or not, nobody thrives for long in an environment where negativity and personal attacks are commonplace. Personal drama kills innovation and creates a culture where people begin undermining each other rather than helping one another. Instill a "no assholes" policy on your team.

FOCUS ON ALIGNMENT. Nothing moves progress sideways and undermines work more than people working together who are not aligned on the project's mission, values, or objective. Make the word *alignment* your North Star and spend time communicating as often as needed on topics that keep your team aligned and not drifting in different directions. Always make sure that the "endgame" result is clear to people and that deadlines are understood and accepted.

GET THE RIGHT PEOPLE ON THE BUS. As Jim Collins describes in the book *Good to Great*, hiring for talent is more important than hiring for positions.[1] If you run into people who are especially talented, aligned personally with your vision and work, and not assholes, hire them. Figure out later the tactical aspects of team integration. Great people make great teams. Implicit in this principle is the idea that you should always be looking for people who are better than you are at key tasks. Good leaders are not threatened by excellence.

GET THE RIGHT PEOPLE IN THE RIGHT SEATS. Having great people on your team is a blessing, but getting them in the "right seats" on the bus is critical—and that may mean different roles for different projects and at different times. The key point is that it's not static; the bus is moving and different things are required at different times. Often, talented people rise to management and stop having time to work on things they really love or were good at. Watch out for this! Disassociate workflow from seniority!

WATCH OUT FOR TITLES. In an ideal world, there would be few, if any, titles within teams suggesting hierarchy and rank because people begin to pigeonhole themselves and others based on this distinction. "That task isn't in my job description" and "Someone at my level should not be doing this" are often complaints that arise from titles.

People on highly effective teams do what needs to be done based on who is best situated to get the work done within the time allowed, and no task is too small. People with experience and talent naturally get tapped for things that use their skills best. The best ideas should win—not necessarily who comes up with them based on rank. Remember, people often rise to the level of their incompetence, so keeping them doing what they are good at is critical.

HIRE FOR DIVERSITY. Despite the claims of people on the political right, hiring and promoting for diversity is not charity. It simply makes for better teams and better work product, and there is a ton of data backing that up. People with different backgrounds bring a wider perspective and a more holistic set of information to any process. New ideas and new energy are often created when there is gender balance as well as diversity of racial and cultural backgrounds and how people identify themselves. It might be easier to get "alignment" when everyone looks and sounds the same, but it's much more powerful when alignment happens through diverse perspectives.

UNDERSTAND HOW YOUR TEAM WORKS. A lot of tools are available these days for assessing the different ways that people learn, communicate, and work—and these can be helpful in honing your team's productivity. We all know that there are introverts and extroverts, for example, but people are much more complex than that, and the field of neurodiversity is quickly making clear that people learn and process information very differently. Consider using tools like Myers-Briggs or CliftonStrengths, as well as direct conversation, to understand how best to work with the people on your team.

KEEP YOUR TEAM FLOWING. We've already discussed how important momentum and maintaining workflow is to the ¾ baked philosophy, and they are even more relevant for entire teams. The worst thing is for people to be spinning their wheels waiting for others to complete their work or to be holding others back. Your job as a member of a team is to constantly be looking for bottlenecks and barriers to a smoothly flowing process. Checking in consistently with others and communicating what you need and what you are doing is essential to a team in flow. Think back to the idea of momentum surfing and what it might mean for a team.

WEED OUT HALF-BAKED THINKERS. People who only do half-baked work do not belong on your team. If someone consistently delivers bad results and expresses no desire to try to calibrate their efforts to the work required, they will be a moral drain on the team in addition to diminishing the quality of the work. Get rid of them, even if they are well liked, because their attitudes and behaviors will begin to influence others.

HARNESS FULLY BAKED PEOPLE. Unlike half-baked workers, people who overcompensate and overdo everything are, in fact, an important part of a team—they work hard, they care about results, they are good at identifying issues and tasks that need to be addressed, and they can be critical voices for excellence. But as much of this book underscores, they pose serious challenges to team effectiveness as well, and thus they must play very specific roles within teams. In general, they are better "reviewers" than creators, so they're great for quality control. If you are in this category, there's a lot in this book to help you begin to think and act in a ¾ baked fashion even while harnessing your desire and need for fully baked results. Harness perfectionists, but gird against their troublesome impulses.

AIM FOR OPTIMAL TEAM SIZES AND EFFICIENT MEETINGS. Bloated teams lead to inefficiency, waste, and a guaranteed lack of profitability. Teams should always start out lean—adding other resources when they're proven essential, but not before. As this book highlights, work is best done efficiently by a few, then shared quickly with many. This is a secret sauce to the ¾ baked approach. Move fast (which only small teams can do) and then share broadly as early as possible so that work can be refined and improved within the bounds of a deadline.

AVOID DEATH BY MEETINGS. A ¾ baked meeting gets quickly to the essence of what needs to be discussed and decided on and doesn't drag on afterward with tangents and less important topics. Meetings happen only when needed and never for the sake of meeting. Certainly, set recurring meetings in order to block that time on people's calendars, but quickly assess before each one if the meeting is essential, and cancel it if it's not.

MASTER THE ART OF BIRD-DOGGING. "Bird-dogging" is an expression I hadn't heard before moving to the United States, but it's one I've become rather fond of. It can mean different things in different contexts, but generally it means to pursue something with dogged determination. This mindset is key to the ¾ baked process, as it ensures that we get the feedback we need on anything, within a reasonable time period, by staying on top of it. Relentlessly checking in, even if some find it annoying, is important. I'm always amazed when people seem hesitant to check in with others. "Oh, I don't want to bother them" and "I'm sure they're working on it" are two lines that often lead to disappointment. And if you don't get the feedback you need when you ask someone, simply ask someone else!

DON'T ASSUME—ASK. Even really talented people sometimes forget deadlines, misprioritize tasks, and get off-track, so checking in frequently and asking questions—bird-dogging—ensures that they're being held accountable and holding themselves accountable. You should develop this trait within your teams: "Hey, just checking in, how's it going? Do you need help? Are we on track?" are lines of constant inquiry in a high-performance team. Don't wait until official meetings to check in. You have multiple modes of communication these days—use them! We've all heard the adage that "the squeaky wheel gets the grease," but in a ¾ baked team, everyone's wheel is squeaking and people are constantly checking in with each other.

Remote Work, Virtual Work, and Free Address

How and where people work are topics of constant discussion in the workplace nowadays, especially since the pandemic upended work patterns. This subject alone is worthy of an entire book, and there are growing opinions on all sides about it and whether or not there are more benefits to everyone being in the office together. For the purposes of this book, I'll share a few high-level perspectives:

- Nothing is as good as people working together in person. People need other people to bring out the best in them and for mentorship, culture building, and personal growth. Not all encounters can be scripted and done online, regardless of how good Zoom or Teams might be. Aim to get your people together in person as much as possible.

- Hire remote workers for exceptional talent. Some people can only join your teams from other geographies, and if they're truly exceptional you should hire them. But they should be the exception, not the rule. Try to get your remote talent at some point to move closer to the hub of activity.

- Encourage free address. People have different acoustical, visual, and spatial needs depending on the type of work they are doing. Where possible, support people moving around within your office to find optimized locations depending on the task at hand. It might mean working on a deck, in the kitchen, or in a conference room—all in one day. Consider spending only ¾ of your time working at your desk and the remainder in other locations in the office.

- Embrace the commute. Excess commuting can be tough on people and drain a great deal of life energy. When people can't live near their work, they should set up a schedule and framework to minimize the negative impact. But they should also embrace the benefits of commuting, which include a chance to mingle with other people on public transportation and an opportunity to separate home life from work life with proper transitions and opportunities to support small businesses along the way. Twenty to thirty minutes of low-stress commuting is in fact very healthy. If commuting takes over an hour, it becomes demanding.

- Consider the smoke break. Be like the smokers in your work-place, who find time for intermittent breaks to go outside. But instead of puffing away, use this time to get a quick "dose of nature" if you can. Perhaps we can call this the "magic of the ¾ baked break"!

- Change your viewing distance from the computer screen to the horizon, get some fresh air, and watch the world for a few min-utes alone or with a coworker.

- Minimize work from home. While this take might not be popu-lar, I think people should try to minimize working from home. If you're a remote worker, consider finding a coffee shop or WeWork space where you can go to be near others most of the time. Working from home can be very productive at times, and some amount should be supported by highly productive teams, but everyone working alone from their homes is antithetical to excellence for any team-based work. Culture dies when people all work from home. It might be fine for a writer or someone who does solo work, but if your work involves others it is better to mostly be around others—and, yes, even if you're an introvert.

Starting Up a Project the ¾ Baked Way

For any team in nearly every discipline, a project's start—not its finish—is often the most important time in the project's life. Figure 11.1 maps out one possible start-up process to ensure success.

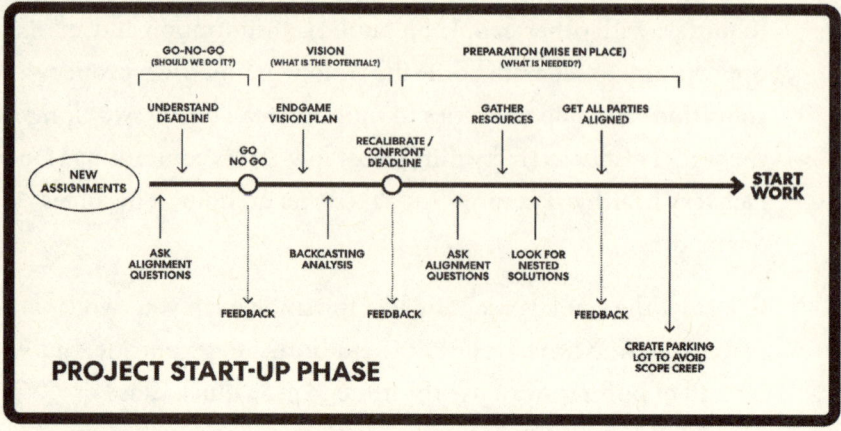

FIGURE 11.1: How a project starts up is critical; this is one proposed approach with key start-up activities.

With any new assignment, there should be a go-no-go phase, where you ask: Should the project be done? How does it align with our mission or values or strategic objectives? Who should do the project or pieces of it? These are all critical alignment questions. What is the deadline? Is it achievable?

Once you've determined that the project is a go, focus in the beginning of the first quarter of the project's life on clearly defining the vision and potential for the project, doing backcasting analysis if appropriate, and recalibrating deadlines and deliverables as needed. This is the vision stage.

After the vision stage, the successful startup requires preparation (mise en place) to gather all necessary resources, get people aligned, and clarify what is in or out of scope to avoid scope creep. Once this is all done, the ¾ baked team is ready to rock and roll (see Figure 11.2).

The start-up process can be quick for effective and time-tested teams, but they never skip the key steps, which put in place the structure to develop innovation and success. Most of your time should be spent on the actual work (not on process), with the focus on testing ideas and learning from failure to bring a project past the ½ baked threshold to the magical ¾ baked moment when it is shared widely.

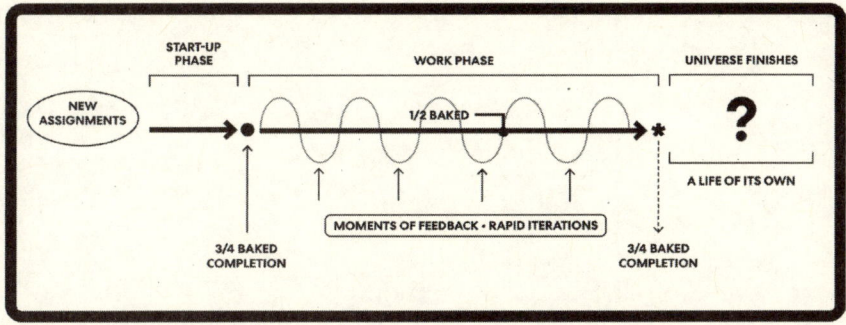

FIGURE 11.2: A flowchart mapping out the ¾ baked process. Most time is spent doing the work and rapidly iterating on it. Then let the universe finish it!

CHAPTER 12

¾ Baked in the Modern Age

*The medium is the message. This is merely to
say that the personal and social consequences
of any medium—that is, of any extension of
ourselves—result from the scale that is introduced into our affairs by each extension of
ourselves, or by any new technology.*

— MARSHALL MCLUHAN

WHEN I STARTED MY CAREER, there were no smartphones, no
email, and no cell phones. In order to check your messages, you had to
go to work and listen to the voicemail on your landline. To respond to
someone, you had to give them a call back, often several times until you
reached them. Phone tag was a very real thing! That's why, when you went
home from work, you mostly left work there. People could not reach you
until the next business day. There was a natural separation between work
life and home life, which was so valuable.

Over the next decade, all of that began to change. Email became commonplace, cell phones and then pagers were quickly adopted, and soon it
became possible for people to reach you at any and all times. I think col-
lectively we all learned some bad habits, not realizing that with any new

technology comes unwanted externalities and the need to establish new societal norms around using them. To make this more challenging, due to the rapidity of technological innovation we're now seeing, each generation is becoming more facile and familiar with new communication styles yet simultaneously losing out on time to develop in-person norms, behaviors, and interpersonal skills. Technological change can be quick, yet culture and individual habits are slow to change. You have people of various generations—boomers, Gen X, millennials, Gen Z—all using the same platforms at work, but with very different contexts, attitudes, and levels of familiarity.

As we've moved next through the adoption of smartphones in the mid-2000s and then from the pandemic of 2019 to 2021 into a world of Zoom, Teams, and online virtual work environments, we've all had to adjust further to significantly different ways of working and communicating. Remote and hybrid work have begun to change a great deal of how we interact with others and get things done. With each change and each new tool, we're promised greater efficiency and gains in productivity—and yet that has rarely been the result.

Instead, we now spend more and more of our time managing our technologies—texts, emails, online chats, and so on—and less time getting work and other important things done. We spend less time in meaningful interactions and more time in virtual ones. We are more connected, yet more clueless.

I remember author and environmentalist Bill McKibben saying that we are "drowning in information and starving for knowledge." But nowadays, we are also drowning in misinformation and starving for truth.

Thanks to the ubiquitous nature of technology, we often trade away our energy on frivolous activities and are poorer for it. Algorithms exist to keep us hooked on spoon-fed content it knows we like, and they distract us from what we should be doing.

Technology is no salve for smart work habits—just a tool that can help or hinder depending on its use and the cleverness of its user. Too often, we become controlled by our technology rather than controlling it. We assume that, because we're busy, we're being effective. Our results typically show the opposite.

So, over the years as I've developed my ¾ baked approach to technology, I've had to learn to use technology, especially communication technology, very efficiently and differently than other people while building guardrails and establishing procedures to enhance my approach. At times, people find my use of technology surprising because with some tools I'm an early adopter and with others I'm a real luddite. This chapter shares a few ideas for you to consider.

Discernment and Technology

The Amish have a philosophy called *Ordnung*, which translates from German to "order, discipline, or rule." But for the Amish, Ordnung more fulsomely refers to the unwritten set of rules and regulations that help them protect their community's long-held traditions. They accomplish this in part with a clear and deep review of any technology to uncover unintended consequences to their way of life and spiritual traditions. If something would undermine these traditions, well, it's banned. In that way, they have held on to nineteenth-century ways of living even while literally surrounded by the trappings of modern life.

In contrast, broader modern society seemingly adheres to the operating philosophy of no restraint whatsoever—other than perhaps the idea that anything new must be better than anything old. We constantly allow new technologies, new chemicals, new ideas to be rolled out without much thought or care about their potential consequences. We've all seen the impacts time and again where things once cherished are lost in the tide of "progress," and where new solutions have served only to create new problems. While I'm not advocating for the level of guardianship that the Amish maintain, we would be wise to be significantly more discerning as a society and as individuals regarding how we let new developments and new technology alter the tried-and-true patterns of our lives.

Take the smartphone, for example. When it was introduced, I was quite excited about it. Finally, there was a device that would bring computing power to my fingertips and connect us all to a great deal of information quickly. I am still excited about smartphones generally, as their capabilities continue to expand in great ways; have you seen the quality of photographs the latest iPhones take? Their storage capabilities are amazing, and some apps are game changers. But smartphones can just as often be a problem, separating us from each other and from community as people spend a large portion of each waking day on their devices.

We've all seen teenagers hanging out and barely talking to each other, instead staring only at their phones. We've all been bombarded by texts and emails at all hours. Instead of focusing on our loved ones and being present in our activities, we scroll and react and keep looking for the constant dopamine hit of instant reactions. The truth is that while these devices are powerful tools, they don't necessarily make us better at much. We now use them to fill all the voids in our time, such that hobbies and personal development often get squeezed instead. People mistake constant connections for lasting relationships and wonder why they are lonelier and more out of touch with others.

Many years ago, I decided to limit the impact that the smartphone was having on my life and the feeling of constantly being connected to the detriment of my family. I took the bold step (as others have described it) of eliminating email from my phone. Nobody needed to be that connected to me. Instead, I have to manually check my email and I do so only at certain points in the day, which allows me to be more focused and present with the rest of my time. The result, while simple, was transformative. I am more on top of my email than nearly anyone I work with, yet I check it less often! I'm more focused during the day than my peers because for every task I do, I'm fully immersed in it rather than trying to multitask and constantly being pulled in different mental directions.

This underscores a critical element of the ¾ baked philosophy: the only way you're going to really do great work and develop the intuition

to know when something is ready to share out into the world is by being present and centered in your work. Someone who is constantly distracted and merely "busy" will miss the subtlety of the approach. Creativity happens through centered application.

On a related note, I rarely give out my cell phone number either, thereby limiting texts to those from people I care to talk to or who are very important to me. The smartphone is mine to use rather than it starting to use me.

Similarly, I've watched a whole range of architectural and graphic design tools be developed over the years, but none, as yet, has proven to be as effective as simply drawing and exploring through sketching. Once my brain has understood a design assignment and its associated three-dimensional challenges enough through a rough sketching process, I can hand it over, ¾ baked, to others to use computer-aided drafting or 3-D modeling software to make it beautiful and compelling. A perfect application of the ¾ baked approach in action! This way, our team is able to create beautiful designs highly efficiently. I have watched others struggle for hours using "advanced tools" to understand something that they could grasp more efficiently by staying "old school" a little longer. Sometimes sticking with tried-and-true approaches is the more effective and efficient approach. Do you always need a cordless drill when a screwdriver still works fine? The answer is that it depends—and that's the difference that discernment makes.

Don't assume that a new tool, technology, or process is better than the old one—test it. Treat tools and technology the same as process. A new tool, like new software, is only good if it truly enhances what you are doing.

The world is about to go through this process again with the introduction of AI and everything it could represent about upending work. In the right hands it might be incredibly useful, but the unintended consequences are barely being discussed and the tech sector is ramping up full-scale implementation regardless. AI is about to change a great deal of society, whether or not we like it—or want it.

Lessons Learned

When using any technology (software, hardware, etc.), apply a layer of skepticism and ask:

- Does it improve the quality of what I'm doing?

- Does it truly improve my ability to communicate?

- Does it make my team more effective?

- Does it really save time overall? In the short term or long term?

- Am I the right one to learn the tool? Or is that best left to others?

- What is the technology truly good for and what are possible undesired side effects?

- Will using the tool take time away from more critical tasks?

Email Hygiene

Few technological tools are as poorly used as email. It has become a challenge for effectiveness, as people rarely make time to discuss how they will use it to communicate effectively. I'm amazed at how many people let their email get out of hand and fall behind with basic communication, now so commonly expected in our work lives. I believe that you can manage email quickly and effectively so that you can spend your time on things that matter the most. To this end, try the following strategies:

- Unsubscribe from any email list you did not sign up for, and stay on top of this. While clutter is hard to avoid completely, keep your inbox as clear as possible.

- Never let your email get backlogged—it is a sign you are holding up others and undisciplined in your approach and means you may miss some key things.

- Check your email at regularly scheduled intervals, not constantly, so that you don't interrupt your mental flow on other tasks. It likely should be every couple of hours at work, or whenever you need a mental break.

- Reply quickly to simple emails when they come in so that they're off your plate and nobody is held up over it. Don't let simple things wait. If you can respond in less than 30 seconds to an email, then do so.

- Do your more thoughtful emails in batches several times a day when you are between other tasks and need a mental break. Otherwise, people find they spend all day going back and forth responding to emails and not focusing on other important work.

- Never write long emails unless absolutely necessary. For anything that requires more than a paragraph or two, pick up the phone or set up a Zoom meeting, or better yet, talk to someone in person. Email is an imperfect communication tool, so don't trust it for something critical or complex. Ask your teams to do the same—ban long emails!

- When you send somebody something important by email, ask for a response or confirmation so you know they got it. This is part of bird-dogging to ensure things flow. Do the same in return: a quick "got it, I'm on it" is reassuring.

- Delegate and forward emails as needed to others. If someone else can respond faster or better than you, let them!

- Never assume that anything you write in an email will not be seen by others. For sensitive topics, talk in person.

- Turn off the noise! Silence notifications. Each time you hear that "ding," it pulls you out of the present, robbing you of centered worktime.

- Remember, nobody deserves twenty-four-hour access to you except possibly your children and your partner.

The World of Zoom

When the pandemic happened and we all had to shelter in place, the business world quickly moved to harness the power of virtual meetings and on-camera huddle-ups.

Videoconferencing was great at first, as it allowed us to see people when we were stuck at home alone all the time. And it's often an improvement over the phone as a communication tool, because it allows us to pick up some body language from other participants, including seeing important facial expressions. It also reduces unnecessary travel or eliminates entire journeys for short meetings, which can now be covered adequately through the technology. These are good things.

But this doesn't mean it's a great approach for most communication—and there is now, for many people, a kind of tyranny of Zoom (or Teams or similar software). Zoom adds yet another layer of things to monitor and stay on top of in addition to email and phone texts. There are also team chats and huddle-up software to vie for our diminishing attention. For many, it has begun to take over a big portion of their daily lives. And this doesn't even account for how much time people spend on social media (TikTok, X, Facebook, Instagram, and LinkedIn). How many virtual relationships can we manage without hurting our real ones? For many people, videoconferencing has also become an excuse for not wanting to go back into a common workplace, even when they should to build team culture and foster better collaboration.

We forget about all the reasons we are supposed to be together— camaraderie, mentorship, and collaboration, to name three. As social creatures who evolved in tribes, it is essential that we have access to the range of verbal and nonverbal cues given off by people we work with. And I would put forward that when you need the input of others—at that ¾ baked moment in particular—it is best shared in person.

The Hierarchy of Communication

As Figure 12.1 explores, the foundation for good communication is always in-person, face-to-face discussions. Without a doubt, you get the most information, direct and indirect, and the greatest psychological and cultural benefits when you meet with someone face-to-face.

As you rise in the workplace pyramid, the nature and effectiveness of the mediums for communication diminish, with email and texts as the least effective. Therefore, seek to prioritize communication and interactions at the base of the pyramid as often as possible.

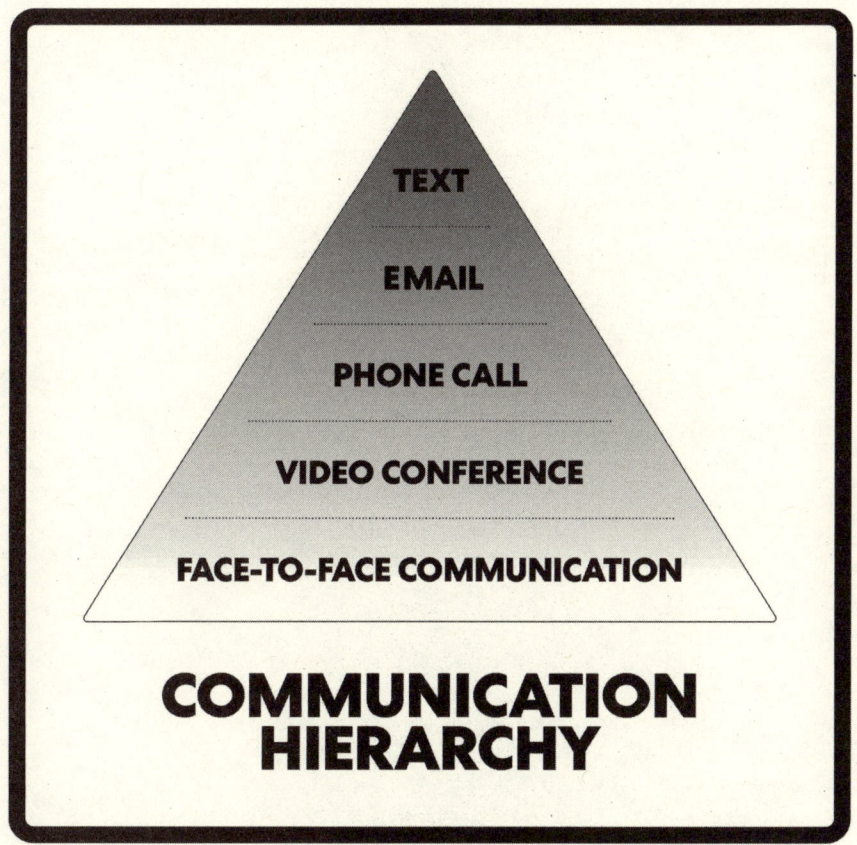

FIGURE 12.1: In the communication hierarchy, nothing beats face-to-face communication. Structure your communication medium based on importance.

CONCLUSION

This Book Is ¾ Baked (An Invitation More Than a Conclusion)

You can't use up creativity; the more you use, the more you have.

—MAYA ANGELOU

NOW THAT WE HAVE come to the end of this book, you can see that it seems quite simple but perhaps not easy. . . .

I'm asking you to think differently, to value your time and that of others around you.

I'm asking you to put your passions first, live your values, and act like what you do matters . . . because it does.

I'm asking you to work smarter, not harder, although to work hard when necessary and to not be afraid to share and collaborate and fail and then fail again—all without getting discouraged, or at least not for long.

I'm asking you to double down when momentum is on your side and to take a break when it's not—take a walk, smell some flowers, do something joyful.

I'm asking you to not take yourself or your ideas so seriously and hold your work so preciously; for god's sake, just get it done already. You have other things to work on regardless of what you are doing now.

I'm asking you to consider whether some things are worth doing at all, and others only barely, so that you save your steam and mettle for the things that matter the most.

I'm asking you to care enough to not put crap out into the world, as lord knows the world is full of it already. No more half-baked work.

I'm asking you to stop chasing perfection, give up being a martyr, and share the credit with those upon whose shoulders you stand and those yet to come, who will only improve upon what you do.

I'm asking you to start being effective and prolific and dependable—and do what you say you're going to do, as the world needs you and your ideas more than ever to count on.

I'm asking you to start the projects of your heart's desires and to stop when they're only ¾ baked, getting your ideas out in the world and setting them free to sink or swim on their own merits.

This is all I'm asking.

Try it!

CONCLUSION—THE SEQUEL

Since the Book Is ¾ Baked, Why Can't I Have Two Conclusions?

AS A FINAL THOUGHT, I wish to speak about *magic* at the end of the book. It is, after all, in the title!

Magic takes many forms in real life—perhaps not the fantastical kind that we read about in fantasy books with conjurings and potions, but something no less impressive in my mind.

The magic that happens when a composer finds a new take on his work when performing in front of others. The magic when an entrepreneur tests something in the market and ends up changing society based on the feedback she gets from users. The magic when we get up after failure, dust ourselves off, and go on to do some of our best work.

This book is in the end an encouragement for you to develop the best version of yourself through the work you do by letting go and not holding on so tightly to what is "perfect" and "right." It's about working hard in service to something greater, even if that something greater is small and personal. It's about opening a door to greater innovation and massive jumps in productivity, allowing you more time to achieve whatever it is that you hope to do.

By embracing imperfection rather than the narrow definition of perfection, we actually open ourselves up to the possibility of future growth, continuous improvement, and collaboration. Ironically and magically, our work gets more and more perfect. Something that is truly perfect, as impossible as that really is, represents a stagnant state that has to be protected. There's no opportunity for growth and only one way for it to go, which is down. How boring is that?!

So embrace your imperfection!

Earlier in the book, I spoke about the inner voice or inner compass that develops as you practice the ¾ baked philosophy. And this is a magical thing indeed to develop. Too often, we are guided by false inner voices—the voices of others and our own fragile egos—that lead us astray by either giving us false confidence in what we're doing or sapping confidence we should in fact have.

As you practice the ideas within this book, the ¾ baked secret is that you'll be developing a more and more accurate internal compass to guide what you do. A voice guided by what is, rather than by what you want (your desires) or hope to avoid (your fears). A more trustworthy compass to guide what you do and how you spend your time. A compass that can help you calibrate your efforts, to know when something is good enough or not, when an idea is half or ¾ baked, and when you need help and when you don't. This compass, which some call "good judgment," isn't something you're born with; it's cultivated through the fires of trial and error, success and failure, that can come only through putting a lot out in the world and being connected to the results. It's an inner trim tab that helps you leverage your own success—to see opportunities clearly for what they are and recognize when to say no or walk away. This inner compass, when calibrated and practiced, will help you get more done in dramatically less time. It will help reduce your stress as you work and allow you to focus on what matters. Once unleashed, it is self-reinforcing as well. As you grow through this process, how you get things done will begin to seem almost magical to others. Let them in on the secrets!

No one's inner compass is ever completely fault free, but when you see someone out in the world who operates at a consistently higher level than others in their field, you can be sure that they have developed it. It came from hard work, not just talent—hard work applied objectively to harness talent.

Watching the tennis great Roger Federer, it is tempting to focus just on his natural talent and how "perfect" his game was and the seemingly effortless way he played. Yes, Federer was incredibly gifted, but there were many other players who were stronger, faster, bigger, and so on. The truth is that Federer made his game as good as it was with the help of a whole team and through his attitude toward improvement. He worked with psychologists on his inner game, with physical trainers on his body, and with multiple coaches and mentors on his shots and strategy. He got better through tough defeats and learned from what he did well. He worked to cultivate his inner compass, which helped him focus on a healthy form of continuous improvement that never dulled his love of the game and his joy of competing. In the game of tennis, Federer's game was a magic of imperfections.

Whatever your game is, I wrote this to help you maintain your love and passion for it by embracing the ¾ baked secret to get your truth out into the world. How do you start? Well, what are you working on now?

THE MAGIC OF IMPERFECTION
DISCUSSION GUIDE

Education is the most powerful weapon you can use to change the world.

—NELSON MANDELA

I HOPE THAT *The Magic of Imperfection* helps you achieve some magical results in your work and life—with greater output and impact but with much less effort. Learning when to let go and share with the world, and accepting the feedback that results, can unlock significant innovation. This discussion guide, organized by chapter, has been designed to help you, your teams, and your organization harness the magic, without trying so darn hard to get everything perfect.

Chapter 1 Dialogue

What do you think holds you back the most in your work?

Do you have big goals or projects in life that you just can't seem to get done? What are they and what's stopping you?

Do you describe yourself as a perfectionist? If so, how does it affect your ability to get work done? If you don't see yourself as a perfectionist, how would you describe yourself? Do you feel like you still do quality work?

Do you know someone who equates their self-worth to the quality of work they do and therefore obsesses over it? Do they seem happy? Why do you think they believe that?

Think about the idea of finding the "sweet spot" with the work you do—what clues can you look for to know when an idea is underbaked versus overbaked as a way of gauging where this sweet spot might be?

Chapter 2 Dialogue

Do you ever take the time to "test your work for failure"? Think of something that you work on that you could rapidly prototype or do quick versions of in order to test whether it's working—it could be a written assignment, a drawing, or something you build. What do you think the result would be?

How early do you share your work with others? Can you imagine sharing it much earlier? Why or why not? What do you think the consequences would be of sharing earlier? What is the worst that could happen?

What was the biggest failure you've had personally or professionally that you learned from? Did it make you a better person or better at what you do?

How do you feel when you "fail" at something? Do you think your reaction is healthy? What would it feel like to separate yourself from failure and to be able to view it objectively?

Chapter 3 Dialogue

When I say "find a mentor, not a hero," why do you think I make that distinction? How would getting advice differ based on how you viewed the person giving you input?

Take a moment to think about who in your life you rely on now to give you feedback on the work you do. Why do you trust them? Are they the best people to give you feedback? Why or why not?

Do you take the time to give good feedback when others ask you for advice or input? What do you think the benefits are of being the provider of feedback and not just the receiver? How might you plan your work in the future to get more feedback at critical stages?

Do you feel like you are too close and attached to your work? When people give you feedback, does it feel like a personal attack or are you able to hear it objectively? How do you think your work would benefit if you were less attached to it and able to hear feedback without taking it personally?

Can you think of an example when you pushed back on some feedback because you knew it wasn't helping the work and an example of when you accepted feedback because it did? What was the difference? Not all feedback is helpful, so how can you develop an inner compass or "honest voice within" to tell the difference?

When you do your work—are you clear on the key main idea or "essence" of the work you are trying to convey? Think back to some recent things you worked on—are you able to describe it in a few words?

Chapter 4 Dialogue

When you dive into work or projects, do you give everything the same level of effort regardless of importance? Why or why not? What drives that strategy within yourself?

Take a look at the significance meter and take time to think about your current workload and how each task would rank on this scale. Anything surprising?

Take a look at the joy/satisfaction meter and take time to rank things you are currently working or focusing on with this meter. Anything surprising?

Now map your current projects and workload on the four quadrants of importance and think about how you might prioritize the work differently than you're currently doing it. Anything you think you should stop working on? Things you should start on right away or prioritize first?

Now take a look at the full dial and pay particular attention to the needle—do you see how it's suggesting you calibrate the level of your effort to importance? Thoughts on how this might affect how you think about work, productivity, and when to share with others?

Chapter 5 Dialogue

When you start a new project, do you always insist on or create a deadline? Why or why not? How can you start to integrate this practice into your daily work?

Think about a time when a colleague let you down by blowing a deadline you were counting on. How did that make you feel? Have you ever done that to one of your colleagues?

Are you someone who procrastinates a lot? Why do you think that's the case? Do you work with others who do as well? What do you notice about how you or they relate to deadlines?

Chapter 6 Dialogue

Think about a time when you were "in the zone" and doing your work felt easy and effortless and fun. Now think about a time when you had to force yourself to get something done and hated the process. Notice how even thinking about each scenario makes you feel. Take time to think about what conditions were present in both those examples that changed how it felt.

Can you list activities or habits you have that tend to break up momentum in your work? What about activities or habits you have that help you keep momentum going? How could you plan to minimize the first and expand the second?

Study Figure 6.1 and think about how it would feel to shorten the troughs and expand the crests. What are some strategies you might practice to do that?

Chapter 7 Dialogue

Do you have a set process for how you do your work or approach things in your life? Where and when did you develop it? Is it working for you? Is it working all the time or just part of the time? Do you think you approach how you do your work out of habit or strategically?

Why do you think that companies and organizations sometimes get bogged down by their own processes and bureaucracy? What do you think can be done in your organization to avoid these same mistakes?

Do you feel like sometimes you or your team have the opposite problem—that is, no set processes or ways of doing things—and you're always reinventing the wheel? Why do you think that is? Do you think there's a balance between taking a consistent approach and needing to adapt your approach to new circumstances or to get different results?

Why do you think some people get just as attached to their process as they do to the work itself? Do you think personal identity gets wrapped up in how people do their work?

Chapter 8 Dialogue

Think about something you are working on or want to achieve right now. What is the "endgame" for the work? What do you want it to achieve? What impact do you want it to have—on whom and what? When do you want the work to be completed?

Are you currently working on things right now without a clear endgame in mind? Do you and your team have a clear vision for what you want to achieve with everything you do? If not, why not? Think about how you might insert thinking about that into the very beginning of your process.

Review Figure 8.2 and think about an example of something you're working on that could benefit from the backcasting approach. Define the endgame vision for the work and when you want it completed, and then create realistic milestones working back from the ultimate deadline. Does this process help you see if your work and timeline are realistic?

Scope creep is a real thing in business and life. People tend to expand a problem or assignment and then have trouble finishing it. Is this something you have trouble with? Why? What about the team you work on? How do you think you can avoid scope creep in the future?

Chapter 9 Dialogue

Have you ever thought about how to apply leverage to the work you do to have greater impact in the world? What do you think that could mean for the type of work you do?

Is there someone you work with or admire that you would call a trim tab thinker? How do they do what they do? What do they do differently than other people?

Take time to think about something you're working on. Can you imagine how the work could have greater impact or meaning or help others? What would need to be different for you to leverage greater change or importance in the world?

Do you see opportunities to work with your competitors or other partners to join forces into larger initiatives? What would this look like? What would the benefits be?

Think about the seven questions asked in the "Steering Yourself Toward Change" section of the chapter. What are your answers?

Chapter 10 Dialogue

Think about the term temporal parasitics. Are there things you do each month that end up consuming large amounts of your time and keep you from doing things you'd really like to do instead? When is the last time you evaluated how you spend your time?

Think about the term temporal dilution. Are there things in your life that fit into that category?

Consider Figure 10.1. How would you adjust these patterns for your life if you were being objective?

Consider Figure 10.2 and Covey's "big rocks" theory of making time first for the important things in your life. Is this something you do now? If not, why not?

Do you use lists to track what you need to get done and to sort their importance and synergies? Consider starting this practice if you aren't! Why do you think the process of making and crossing off things on a list is helpful for so many people? Try creating a list of things you're working on in the format shown in Figure 10.4. Feel free to modify it as you wish!

Do you make enough time for yourself and your loved ones? Or have you got into a pattern of leaving that at the end of your list? Consider the long-term impact of not prioritizing being centered, healthy, and rested and making time for people and things you care about.

Chapter 11 Dialogue

Do you work on a team? Would you consider the team you're working with now a "¾ baked team"? Why or why not? What holds your team back from greatness?

Has your team taken time to study its own dynamics using tools like Myers-Briggs or CliftonStrengths? Consider doing so as a way to see how your strengths and challenges manifest.

Do you have half-baked and fully baked thinkers on your team? Without singling people out, why do you think that? Do you have the right people "on the bus" and "in the right seats"?

Consider the idea of the ¾ baked meeting and the ideal meeting size as you plan your next meeting. How do you find the sweet spot for who to include and how long to meet?

When do you use technology to meet virtually, and when do you meet in person? Why? With what frequency? What works best for you and your team?

Chapter 12 Dialogue

How do you use technology to do your work? How has it changed over the years? Has your work become better or worse or been unaffected by technological progress? In what ways?

How do you evaluate what new tools, hardware, software, or technology to introduce into your life and your work? Think about new tech you may have recently started using—is it doing what was promised?

Do you stay on top of your email, or does email seem to overwhelm you? Have you thought about changing your practices around electronic communication? If so, what do you think you could do differently for better results?

THE DNA OF THE PROBLEM MAKERS

*Keep away from people who try to belittle
your ambitions. Small people always do that,
but the really great make you feel that you,
too, can become great.*

— MARK TWAIN

CERTAIN PERSONALITY TYPES OR TRAITS have a particular challenge with the ¾ baked philosophy in action. You might recognize one or more of these traits in yourself or your colleagues, so it's useful to understand how to overcome them. In this appendix, I identify six personality types that have a hard time enacting the ¾ baked process: the Perfectionist, the Expander, the Contrarian, the Egoist, the Procrastinator, and the Plodder. I provide tips on how to identify them and how to perhaps begin to work with them. And, of course, as complex beings, people might be more than one of these at any one time or different combinations at different times. This appendix identifies six "types" that have particular difficulty with ¾ baked thinking.

The Perfectionist

We all know what it means to be a perfectionist. Everything must be perfect for these individuals and so work gets revisited, re-edited, and redone over and over again. A perfectionist is hesitant or downright resistant to sharing what they are working on. When they do get things done, it can be fantastic! But generally, it takes the individual so much effort and time to complete anything that their output suffers and deadlines are often missed or met only at great cost to the perfectionist or others around them. Perfectionists are often walking examples of burnout waiting to happen. Who wouldn't get frustrated trying so hard and seemingly having so little to show for it?

If You Are a Perfectionist

Perfectionists need to let things go and rein in their need for everything to be perfect. In fact, they need to actively learn that sometimes greater things come out of imperfections and rely on others to help "perfect" something rather than doing it all themselves.

If You Manage a Perfectionist

Use perfectionists wisely. They are best suited to helping edit or improve others' work since they do not self-identify with it as much, and their tendencies for refinement can be put to good use. Give them a copy of this book! Help them understand how giving up more control and sharing earlier ultimately helps them reach their goals sooner.

The Expander

An expander, also known as a drifter, is someone who lacks the discipline to stick with the core or essence of any particular project. Despite good intentions, what an expander sees is not clarity of purpose but instead the field of possibilities. The expander takes any assignment and keeps adding to it, thus making every problem bigger, more complex, and ultimately harder to finish as a result. Left to their own devices, an expander will drift around as things catch their interest and sometimes solve everything except for the original assignment or work to be completed! Ultimately, even with great talent, expanders can frustrate others around them, since they can't seem to stay on the same page as others or get things done in a timely fashion. When you work hard but on the wrong things, the results are still failed effort.

If You Are an Expander

Expanders need to acknowledge that a shortage of ideas is not their problem. Instead, they should jot down ideas as they arise and put the ideas in a "parking lot" for future exploration **once they finish the assignment or project as intended.** In this way, good ideas aren't forgotten, but they don't disrupt progress in the here and now. Revisited later, truly good ideas will lead to new things worth doing.

If You Manage an Expander

Your job is keeping them aligned. Expect to babysit them more than others to keep them on track and focused. You'll need the patience to deal with their tendency to drift and the willingness to review and acknowledge new things they bring to the table. Expanders are great for early conceptual work to help you identify new ideas, solutions, and perspectives. If the perfectionist can be harnessed as a "closer," the expander is a good "starter."

The Contrarian

It is impossible to go about business and not meet the contrarian personality type. This is an individual who pokes at everything, looking for the flaw or challenge or problem with any initiative or piece of work. Seeing only negatives, they can often miss solutions and lack the courage to try approaches that are new and innovative. They are often morale killers on a team as they don't know how to stop and enjoy progress or celebrate their own or others' success. When you only see the downside, it is challenging to learn from what's working and to view things objectively. This individual is often unable to get anything done because they become paralyzed by what-ifs. They see themselves as pragmatists or realists when they're just viewing the world through a half-empty perspective. Negativity rarely produces greatness.

If You Are a Contrarian

Are you not tired of yourself? Do you not see others enjoying life and having fun doing things, and do you not want to quiet that critical and fearful inner voice? The contrarian needs to take a critical look in the mirror and understand the impact they are having on themselves and the people around them. They need to remind themselves to try to be more positive in group situations.

If You Manage a Contrarian

It's important to manage contrarians, or they'll hurt team morale. Find out what motivates or drives their negativity and see if it can be assuaged. Ask them to try first acknowledging the challenges in something, then taking a leap of faith and working on it as if it is positive, even if they worry it won't be. Contrarians can be useful in strategic planning to help you identify blind spots and challenges to solve. Help them learn to celebrate successes of others and themselves and to understand the impact of their negativity. However, if they can't ever see the positive, they might need an entirely different role or job.

The Egoist

Egoists see the world through the lens of their own personal value, identity, and need for attention. They are often ambitious and can in fact work very hard, sometimes to great result, but the work they do tends to reflect on themselves rather than to serve the work itself or benefit others. For certain types of work, like solo or artistic or athletic pursuits, this might be fine, but for anything that requires teamwork or group contributions, it's a recipe for failure. The egoist will prioritize tasks that make them look or feel better over what is best for the project. They won't hesitate to undermine others or the work itself if doing so gets them what they want. There is little to no dedication to getting things done if the work begins to be tiresome or challenging in any way to the individual's fragile ego.

If You Are an Egoist

You likely are not reading this book! If you are, you should view this as an opportunity to get even further in your goals and to become even more effective.

If You Manage an Egoist

Good luck! Sometimes you can leverage the egoist to great effect by ensuring that they remain personally invested in anything they are doing. By feeling ownership over the work, they stay motivated to make things better—just be ready to share or give credit! Showing this personality how they benefit from the ¾ baked philosophy can be effective in harnessing great things, provided you can put up with them!

The Procrastinator

The procrastinator is known to us all—and most of us have tendencies at times to be one. They have a hard time committing to things and really struggle with a blank page at the start of assignments. This individual is good at finding other things to work on rather than the key assignment. They are not necessarily afraid of hard work but struggle to know how to begin and where to build momentum. They benefit the most from learning to surf for momentum.

If You Are a Procrastinator

Try to practice by recognizing this tendency in yourself and really doubling down on the "order of operations" process described in this book. I'm convinced that procrastinators can be cured of their tendencies the more they see results from what they work on.

If You Manage a Procrastinator

These individuals struggle with starting things, but they can be good contributors when they're not asked to frame up new assignments and start at the beginning. Pair them up with others who are less afraid of the blank page and have them work on things that are easy to dive into until they can build their own momentum.

The Plodder

The plodder is not a very glamorous personality type to have on a team, but sometimes they are required to get a job done. By definition, a plodder works hard and at their own pace—which is typically very slow. They have trouble with expansive visions that do not clearly show a path from point A to point B. They struggle with seeing the "essence" in work and respond better to more pragmatic tasks because they pride themselves on being pragmatists. It can be challenging to get them to work faster, but they will always move an assignment forward if given the chance.

If You Are a Plodder

It's okay to admit that you're a plodder and to work on things that play to your strengths. Accept that you're not the "idea person" and work hard to make other ideas stronger through execution and persistence. You can become a very valuable part of any team.

If You Manage a Plodder

Accept them for what they are and harness their strengths to help execute detailed and careful work. Figure out what they're good at and give them assignments that allow them to put their heads down and focus. Plodders don't do well if put in charge as they become bureaucratic quickly, but given important tasks and recognition, they are motivated to do solid work for any team.

NOTES

Chapter 3

1   Brett Lovelady, "Design Is a Point of View: Seven Truths in Designing," *Fast Company*, July 10, 2009, *https://www.fastcompany.com/1307125/design-point -view-seven-truths-designing*.

Chapter 9

1   In recent years, green teams have sprouted up in almost every major firm. Elements was the first of its kind.

Chapter 10

1   Betty Edwards, *Drawing On the Right Side of the Brain*, 4th ed. (New York: TarcherPerigree, 2012).

2   Vicki Robin and Joe Dominguez, *Your Money or Your Life: 9 Steps to Transforming Your Relationship with Money and Achieving Financial Independence* (New York: Penguin, 2008).

3   If you're wondering why this doesn't add up to twenty-four hours, keep in mind that these are all averages from various sources and not from a real person. Each person's mix, based on current understanding of time and physics, would add up to twenty-four hours. There may also be some "double counting," as people tend to do multiple activities at once, such as eating while watching TV.

4   Stephen R. Covey, *7 Habits of Highly Effective People* (New York: Free Press, 1989).

5   Thich Nhat Hanh, *The Miracle of Mindfulness: An Introduction to the Practice of Meditation*, trans. Mobi Ho (Boston: Beacon Press, 1999).

Chapter 11

1   Jim Collins, *Good to Great: Why Some Companies Make the Leap . . . and Others Don't* (New York: Random House Business, 2001).

ACKNOWLEDGMENTS

I WISH TO THANK a few people who have helped shape this book into what it is today:

To my wife, Tracy McLennan, for cheering me on as I worked through the manuscript.

To my father, Dr. Fred McLennan, for early reviews and encouragement.

To Jay Torell, who helped me with the graphics for the book.

To Mary Thomas, who helped develop a few of the concepts and stories repurposed from my previous book, *Zugunruhe: The Inner Migration to Profound Environmental Change.*

To David Trubridge, who contributed a case study and a diagram as well as design inspiration.

To the International Living Future Institute, its board, and its staff, for being the test ground for many of my ideas getting out into the world.

To my colleagues and staff at McLennan Design and Perkins&Will, who continue to let me test my theories on our practice every day.

And finally, to the great team at Berrett-Koehler Publishers, especially my editor, Steven Piersanti, who helped with all aspects of this publication.

INDEX

ABOUT THE AUTHOR

EARLY ON IN HIS CAREER, JASON F. MCLENNAN learned that having influence meant getting ideas out in the world and working hard regardless of the initial chance of success. Through relentless practice over the last three decades, he has learned how imperfection can magically become the shortest path to actual perfection and positive change in the world.

Trained as an architect and urban planner, he learned early that failure and critical feedback, if properly utilized, led to better and better work. He learned to harness his perfectionist nature in order to calibrate his efforts to the importance and nature of the task and to iterate quickly and effectively in order to achieve innovative results.

The result is that he is now considered one of the world's most influential individuals in the field of architecture and green building movement, sought out around the world as a designer, consultant, and thought leader. He is the recipient of the prestigious Buckminster Fuller Prize (the planet's top prize for socially responsible design). He has been called both the Steve Jobs and Wayne Gretzky of the green building industry, was designated a "World Changer" by *GreenBiz* magazine, and won the National Award of Excellence from *Engineering News-Record*—one of the few individuals in the architecture profession to have won the award in its sixty-year history.

More than an architect, however, McLennan applied his ¾ baked philosophy of innovation to help shape the entire design and construction industry, in rapid succession releasing tools, programs, and standards that redefined sustainability. McLennan is the creator of the Living Building Challenge—the most stringent and progressive green building program in existence, as well as a primary author of the WELL Building Standard, which is sweeping the globe. He created the industry's first "red list" for building materials and its associated DECLARE label, shaping chemistry and materials ingredients in thousands of products used all over the globe. He created JUST, the first social justice transparency program to help companies live their values according to clear and transparent metrics. He created the first net-zero energy and zero carbon standards used in the building industry and more recently created GOAL, a program designed to hold sports venues—including in the NHL, NBA, and NFL—to a higher sustainability standard.

He is the author of seven books on sustainability and design used by thousands of practitioners each year, including the *Philosophy of Sustainable Design*, considered the "bible for green building," and is both an Ashoka Fellow and Senior Fellow of the Design Future's Council.

McLennan has also applied his magic of imperfection approach to starting businesses and not-for-profits—including being the founder of the International Living Future Institute and the School of Regenerative Design, Ecotone Publishing, and McLennan Design. He was selected by *Yes! Magazine* as one of "15 people shaping the world" and works closely with world leaders, Fortune 500 companies, leading NGOs, major universities, celebrities, and influential development companies—all in the pursuit of a world that is socially just, culturally rich, and ecologically restorative.

McLennan is currently serving on the board of the International Living Future Institute and is the principal of McLennan Design and chief sustainability officer for Perkins&Will, the world's second largest architecture firm, designing some of the planet's most advanced green buildings. His work has been published in dozens of journals, magazines, and newspapers around the world. He has a deep passion for helping everyone exceed their potential and share their gifts of creativity in a world that needs every good idea it can get.

Berrett–Koehler
Publishers

Berrett-Koehler is an independent publisher dedicated to an ambitious mission: *Connecting people and ideas to create a world that works for all.*

Our publications span many formats, including print, digital, audio, and video. We also offer online resources, training, and gatherings. And we will continue expanding our products and services to advance our mission.

We believe that the solutions to the world's problems will come from all of us, working at all levels: in our society, in our organizations, and in our own lives. Our publications and resources offer pathways to creating a more just, equitable, and sustainable society. They help people make their organizations more humane, democratic, diverse, and effective (and we don't think there's any contradiction there). And they guide people in creating positive change in their own lives and aligning their personal practices with their aspirations for a better world.

And we strive to practice what we preach through what we call "The BK Way." At the core of this approach is *stewardship,* a deep sense of responsibility to administer the company for the benefit of all of our stakeholder groups, including authors, customers, employees, investors, service providers, sales partners, and the communities and environment around us. Everything we do is built around stewardship and our other core values of *quality, partnership, inclusion,* and *sustainability.*

We are grateful to our readers, authors, and other friends who are supporting our mission. We ask you to share with us examples of how BK publications and resources are making a difference in your lives, organizations, and communities at bkconnection.com/impact.

Dear reader,

Thank you for picking up this book and welcome to the worldwide BK community! You're joining a special group of people who have come together to create positive change in their lives, organizations, and communities.

What's BK all about?

Our mission is to connect people and ideas to create a world that works for all.

Why? Our communities, organizations, and lives get bogged down by old paradigms of self-interest, exclusion, hierarchy, and privilege. But we believe that can change. That's why we seek the leading experts on these challenges—and share their actionable ideas with you.

A welcome gift

To help you get started, we'd like to offer you a **free copy** of one of our bestselling ebooks:

bkconnection.com/welcome

When you claim your **free ebook**, you'll also be subscribed to our blog.

Our freshest insights

Access the best new tools and ideas for leaders at all levels on our blog at ideas.bkconnection.com.

Sincerely,

Your friends at Berrett-Koehler